RANDALL KNIVES

Rare, Unique & Experimental

Turner
PUBLISHING COMPANY

Nashville, Tennessee • Paducah, Kentucky

Turner Publishing Company
200 4th Avenue North • Suite 950   412 Broadway • P.O. Box 3101
Nashville, Tennessee 37219   Paducah, Kentucky 42002-3101
(615) 255-2665   (270) 443-0121

www.turnerpublishing.com

Copyright © 2006 Robert E. Hunt

Publishing Rights: Turner Publishing Company

This book or any part thereof may not be reproduced or transmitted in any form or by any means, electronic or mechanical, including photocopying, recording, or by any information storage and retrieval system, without permission in writing from the authors and the publisher.

Library of Congress Control Number: 2006900582

ISBN: 978-1-63026-943-2

0 9 8 7 6 5 4 3 2 1

Contents

Section I: Randall Museum Knives *11*

Section II: "Experimental" Randall Knife Collection *73*

Section III: Rare and Unique Knives *111*

Index *175*

In Appreciation

The unique, rare and experimental content of this book could not have been effectively compiled without the willing and enthusiastic support of Gary T. Randall. True to the principles established by his father, Gary has steered the business, in part or whole for forty years. RMK today, as at its inception, makes knives to be used by contemporary customers. Its total focus is directed toward this goal. They do not collect Randalls. In spite of this, the company has "withstood" the remarkable rise of collector interest in knives built by them decades ago. Gary has accommodated this phenomenon and taken it in stride, while never losing sight of the reality of the business. He should be congratulated for both his steadfastness in meeting the ongoing demands for their fine cutlery, as well as supporting individual and group interests in "historic" Randall knives.

Sara Hunt has been constant in her support and encouragement throughout the building of these three books. During what has amounted to a five year time span, that support has been essential in accomplishing the final result.

Once again, Paul Liebenberg has made significant contributions reflected in the photographic enhancements seen on the pages of this book, which were achieved through the accommodation of the best of both film and digital technology. Paul has supplied the necessary experience and skill that allowed us to get out of the studio and shoot in the field. The project would have been impossible to complete using the "old ways". During the process, Paul provided support and advice that carried over into other aspects of the publication as well. For insights into Liebenberg's technical accomplishments in the pistol building field, see his website, www.pistoldynamics.com.

Julie Murkette, who manages my website, www.randall-collector.com, has once again prepared the text for final submission to the publisher. Her many skills in the fields of design and typesetting, copyediting, and web page design are described on her website, www.juliemurkette.com.

I would like also to acknowledge the many friends who share the same collecting interest and who interact with the author on a regular basis, providing insights, opinions, information, enthusiasm; who share tables at shows, exhibit their knives and, in short, make the experience a rewarding one.

Finally, I extend my gratitude to the Randall collectors who have graciously sent knives from their collections, to be photographed for this book. Their contributions are important to the publication and appreciated by the readers. Their names appear along with the images of their knives.

Dedication

This book is dedicated to the memory of Pete Hamilton.

Between the writing of this publication and its release, we have witnessed the passing of Pete Hamilton, former and longtime Randall Shop foreman. In his capacity at the shop, Pete made hundreds of friends and served as the "recognizable" individual interacting with the public in that very busy workplace. It was during one of those contacts, about fifteen years ago, that the author found that he and Pete had several things in common. That began a long period of communication, which grew out of respect and admiration for Pete as an individual. Many others have shared the experience, but many may not be writing a book on the subject of Randall Knives and perhaps won't have the opportunity to make their feelings known in so public a manner. He will be missed both as a friend and an expert in his field who was a knowledgeable, willing and cheerful ambassador for Randall Made Knives.

– Robert E. Hunt

Introduction

If there is a theme in this volume, it is identification with W.D. Randall's continuous design innovation, cataloged here in part by the appearance of images that often reflect the step by step enhancement of prototypical experimental knives.

It has been reported that Bo, in many cases, made an additional knife for the museum when he had been asked to provide the customer with a type unique to his current line. In photographing these knives and scrutinizing many others that do not appear in this volume, it became apparent that there was more method in the process than mere duplication of a customer's order. Many examples represent otherwise undocumented steps in the process from raw design to completion. This is important as it both indicates and underlines experimentation.

Some of these early "experiments" archived in the museum, eventually made an appearance as a derivative of an established model, although perhaps never becoming a catalog offering. These latter types are seen in examples photographed and described in Section Two. Additionally, common characteristics are identifiable throughout the entire volume, sometimes in handle style, or blade type or in a final finished knife itself.

The stiletto, (a favorite design of the author), was undoubtedly a favorite of W.D. Randall. In many photographs we can see Bo with a stiletto in his hand. An early letter depicted in Randall Military Models, in Bo's own handwriting, declares that the "Commando" knife came first, followed by the #2 and then the #1. We all know that the stiletto wasn't the first introduced, but there were certainly many Fairbairn-Sykes commando knives circulating around at the outset of WWII. It would be naïve to believe that they remained "undiscovered" by the most innovative knife maker in America. That the fighter (an American design) made the first appearance of the two, was due to the influence of Zacharias and one or more other aggressive customers who drove the type and design, so that it materialized as a completed project earlier than the stiletto (a British design). The hypothesis is the author's, but it doesn't contradict the facts. Further, the museum knives are well represented by Randall's "innovative" stiletto designs. They also appear in other sections of the book. The reader should be drawn to their distinct features. The majority of the knives depicted, however, are a representative assortment; some fighters, some hunters, some Bowies and some very convincing full-tangs. Although not all inclusive, we have selected a strong sampling of those displayed in the Randall Museum.

Photographing the museum knives individually provides us with a first-time view of pieces heretofore only seen grouped in a display case. This was a compelling factor in producing the section. The "stand alone" knife does not have a sheath to rely on and reveals all of its features without props or complimentary compositions. Thereby, each example's unique character is established for the reader.

The publishing of this book signals the culmination of a project spanning five years and represents countless hours of study and some original research. Throughout its course, and with the cooperation of many collector friends, we have examined scores of knives of many models. This has served to speed up the learning process, as well as provide the confidence necessary to accurately write supporting text for knives designed and produced as long ago as sixty-five years.

Section I:
Randall Museum Knives

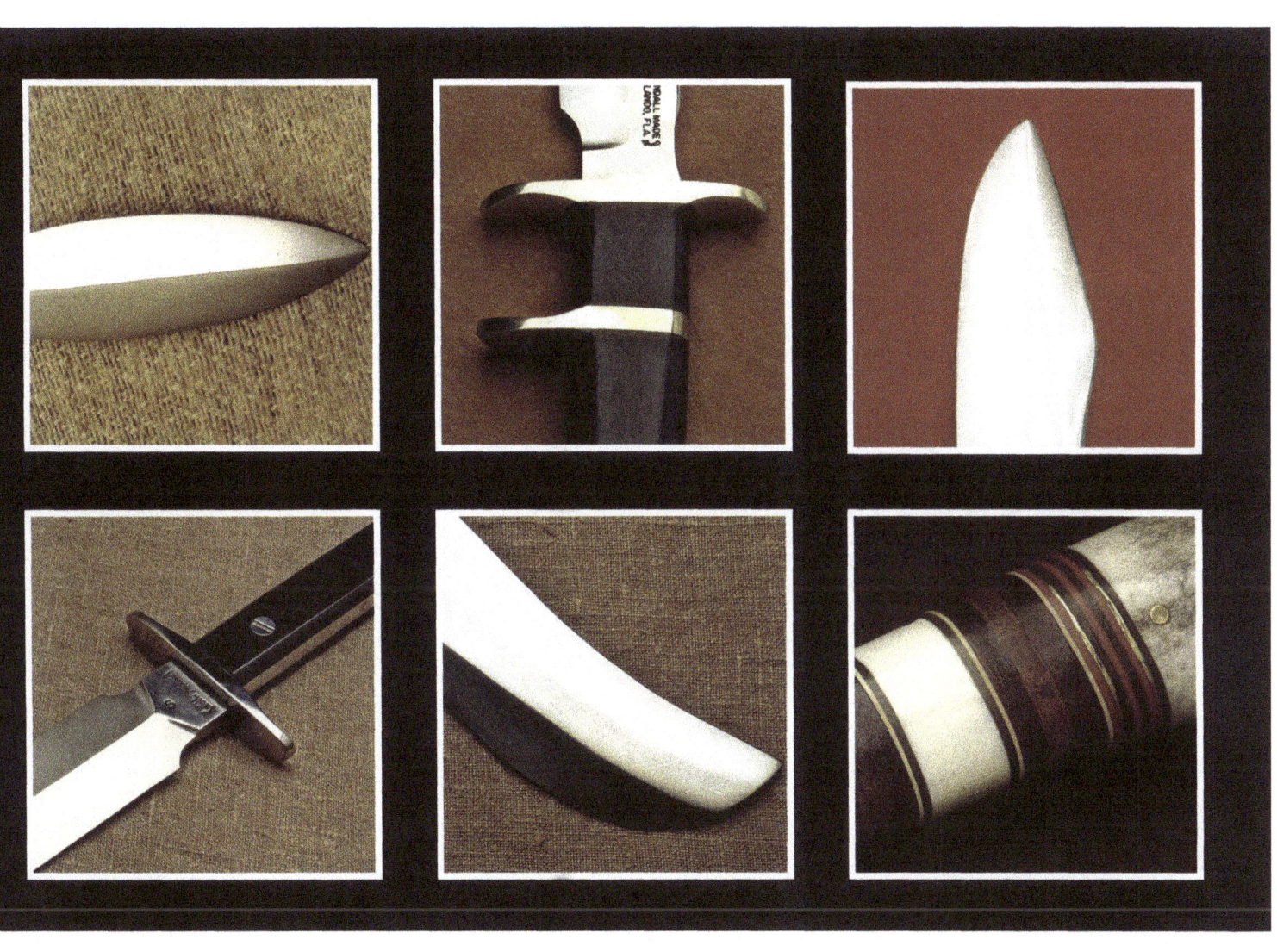

Early 1940s Fighter

This early Fighter with 6-inch blade was favored by the maker and bears his name. Note the location, as later examples were name etched on the reverse side of the blade. This logo, incorporated during 1939, indicates time of production. Leather handle washers were introduced at the end of 1942 and the spacer arrangement shows a metal as well as fiber arrangement. This is a handsome example of one of Bo's first fighters and yes, in this case, most assuredly made by him.

1940s Fighter
Reverse curved upper guard

The cover of Randall Fighting Knives in Wartime features a similar knife, along with its original sheath. This example, which is displayed in the museum, is identical and exhibits the same innovation on the upper guard extension. The forward angle facilitated thumb placement, a gripping position favored by Bo.

Other characteristics are attributed to very early 1940s production: the spacers, thick leather handle washers, very thin butt cap, flat blade grind and location of the trademark.

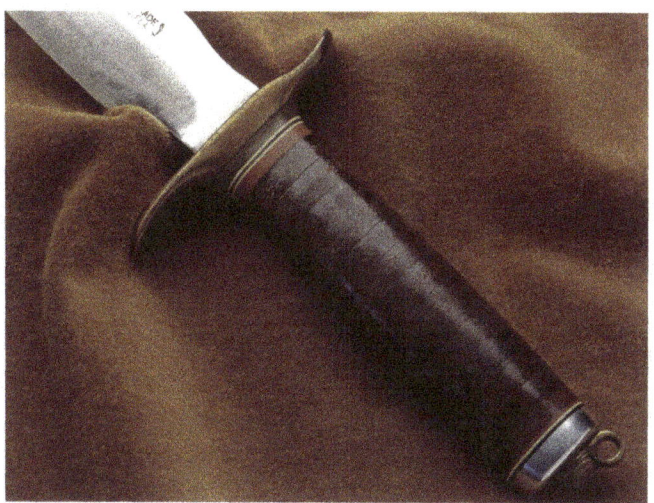

World War II Fighter
8" blade

We can go on forever writing about this knife. Although not the first Randall Fighter (style), it nonetheless represents the type universally recognized, with wrist thong clip, handle shape and spacer arrangement. What's more, it provides the viewer with a "new-appearing" example, underlying the attraction and appeal of the model to its contemporary users.

Like all the knives in this section, it is depicted without a sheath. Although not commonly known, some museum examples were originally provided with sheaths, but they were stored separately due to lack of space in the display cases.

Randall Commando

The flowing lines of the "Commando" are distinctive and represent one of Bo's attempts at a fighter design. The initial commandos can be traced back to perhaps 1942, although this one appears to be of later production (note the absence of a tang nut and the logo stamping). Upstaged by the Zacharias fighter, which became the prototype for the Model #1 fighter, this style never seriously competed for a place in the catalog. Its origin and design favor the hunter type and provide an important link to the evolution of the Randall blade type.

Styers Fighter

The principles of knife fighting advanced by Styers are reflected in the ultimate design represented in this fighter, the prototype being a late 1950s cut down tang Model #14 with "S" shaped hilt. He was an advocate of the Biddle methods utilized in the USMC during the 1930s and 40s, which eventually led to the formulation of his specific fighting technique later adopted by the Corps.

Bo and Styers met during the USMC equipment Board tests in the mid-1950s. They became friendly and then collaborated on this design. The distinctively contoured hilt was Styers' idea for indexing the thumb and is just another example of Randall's diverse interests in knife utility and design. Note the "S" shaped guard and modified commando handle with drop.

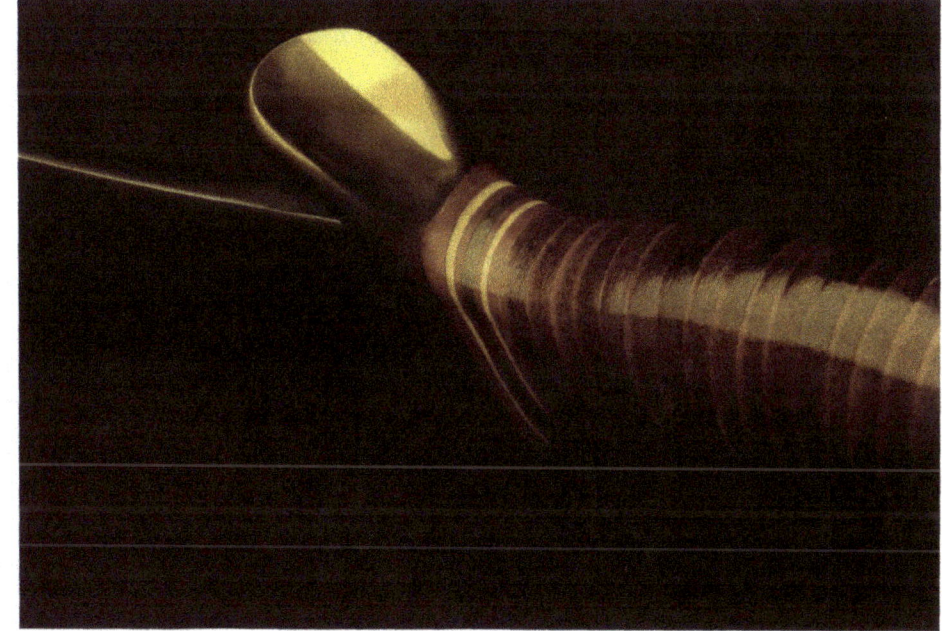

Sub-Hilt Fighter
6" Blade

Bo Randall initially experimented with sub-hilt fighters as early as the 1950s; they appear on fighters and Bowies alike. This example with micarta handle was made much later, perhaps during the 1970s. The guard and sub-hilt appear to be nickel silver and together they facilitate finger placement for a particular manner of presenting the blade.

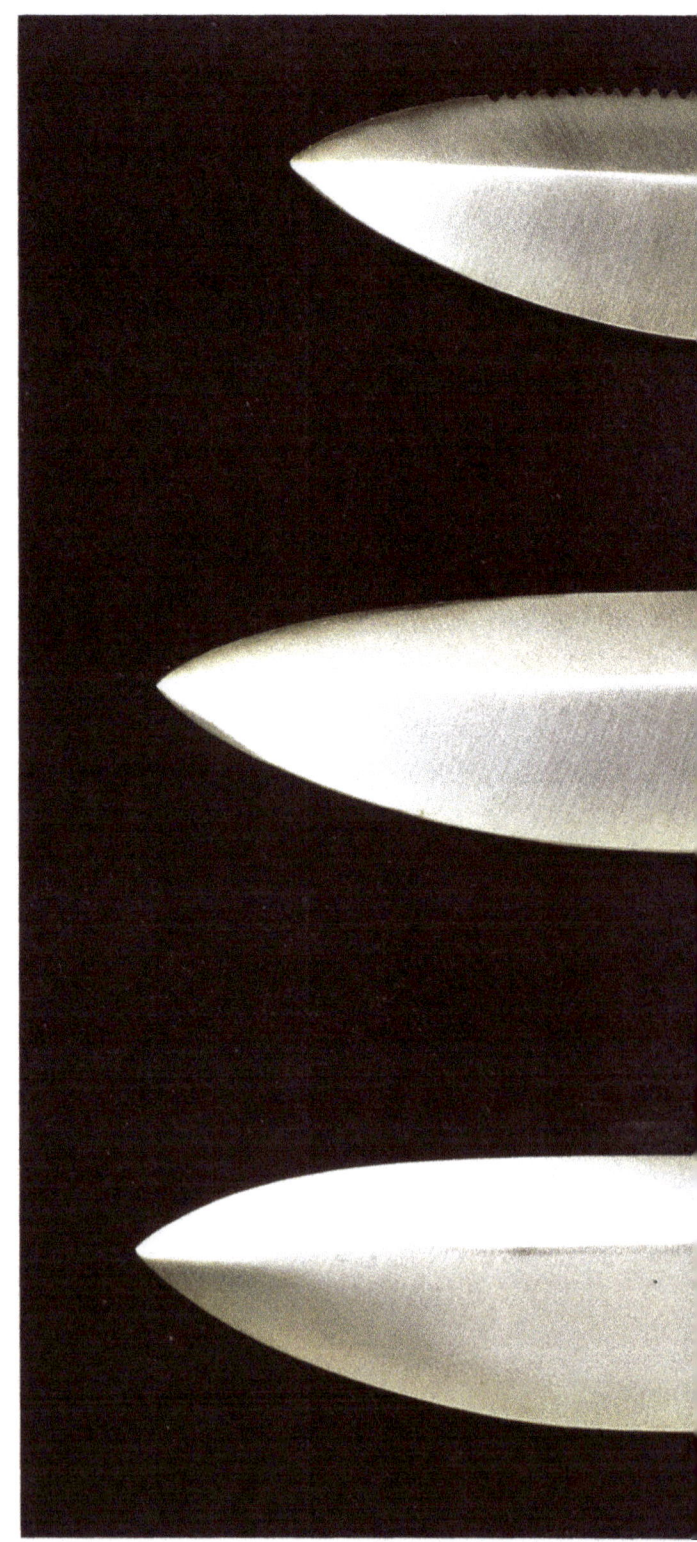

Special Stilettos

These images represent prototype full tang modified stiletto blades with "Astro" cavity. They are experimental survival types produced prior to the hollow handle Model #18. Note the low "s" location. The center knife has a forward curved half-guard and the upper saw teeth; the lower with a brown micarta handle in place. Unlike some examples, these prototypes were destined to reach the completed knife stage and a finished pair appears in the second section of this book.

Fairbairn Ivory Stiletto

Here is a 1950s era double-pinned ivory commando style handle with small guard and narrow blade. Each knife photographed for this chapter evoked a pause during set-up, but none quite drew the photographer's attention and appreciation so much as this beautifully contoured stiletto; clearly a Fairbairn type, modified by the Randall touch. Paul was heard to say that "if I could have just one…" and the author concurs. If this project should achieve any success, it will be connected with the presentation of each knife individually, isolated from the display case, standing alone without reliance on sheath or composition.

Full Tang Stiletto with Long Guard
7" Blade

This image represents a reoccurring theme of the stiletto in evolution and another example of a full tang Model #2. Bo's interest in the stiletto as a blade type is reflected in its various modifications, which serve to satisfy the requirements and demands of the period.

The long cross guard on this knife is brass, brazed to the tang. The contour of the handle favors that of fine antique dinner cutlery. The date of production is unknown, but like most other museum examples, it represents early experimentation.

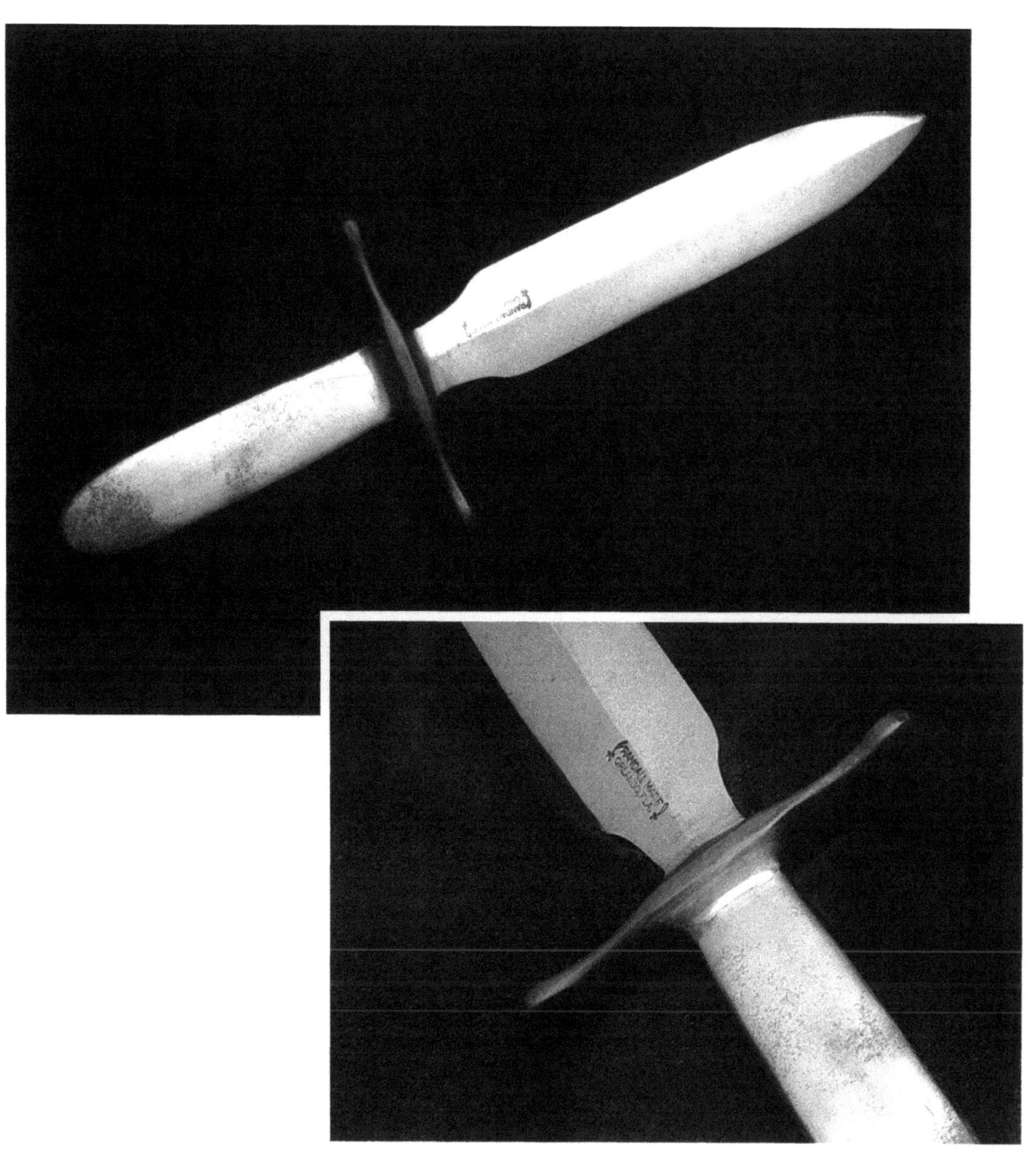

Wide Blade Stiletto
6½" Blade

Two screws hold the brown micarta handle slabs in place on this knife, another example of an attempt by Bo Randall to accommodate and utilize the then recently introduced "Astro-type" handle cavity on a full tang stiletto with broad blade. Again we see the stiletto blade carrying the innovation. Observe the wide blade, strengthened ricasso with logo stamp and flat guard design of the full tang models.

Choiless Stiletto
5½" Blade

This uniquely ground stiletto was made along with two dozen more to commemorate a Randall family reunion in Colorado and the serial numbered knives were passed out as gifts.

A lingering glance allows us to identify several unusual characteristics not available on standard Model #2s. Note the shape of the burl handle and butt cap. The guard is reduced to balance the blade and handle. The result is a very accommodating little dagger.

7" Carved Ivory-handled Stiletto
Macro Handle

This knife appears to have a standard blade, guard and handle shape, although the material used on the latter is ivory and the checkering done by Leschorn. Observe the initial plate. One dissimilar characteristic is the treatment of the butt cap, which is grooved and carries a large nut. This is one of the few museum knives that shows use, which may in part be attributed to Bo's preference for the model as a letter opener.

35

7" Malaysian Kris

This blade style originated in Indonesia and has cultural roots in the region. The uneven and wavering blade design has been attributed to many things, including a snake, and the knife style itself has been used for all sorts of purposes over the centuries, including battle.

This example must have required unusual forging and grinding procedures that undoubtedly led to its rarity.

Jade-handled Stiletto

This knife was produced during the late 1960s while the shop was experimenting with jade handle material. Note the grooved and flat-sided commando style handle. The guard is nickel silver along with the butt cap. The 6" stainless blade carries a separate "s".

Model #14
7½" — Prototype knife

This "Attack" model is the prototype knife submitted to the USMC Equipment Board for evaluation during their testing period in 1954. The nylon handle is held in place with three bolts and the blade and guard are chromed. The strength of design in its image of a Model #1 can be readily seen in this full tang revision of the famous fighter. The first and lasting impression on the two Marine Corps representatives was very positive, despite the Board's failure to select a knife for their Air Crews and pilots.

This prototype is a compelling design even when viewed today and the model continues its popularity a half-century later.

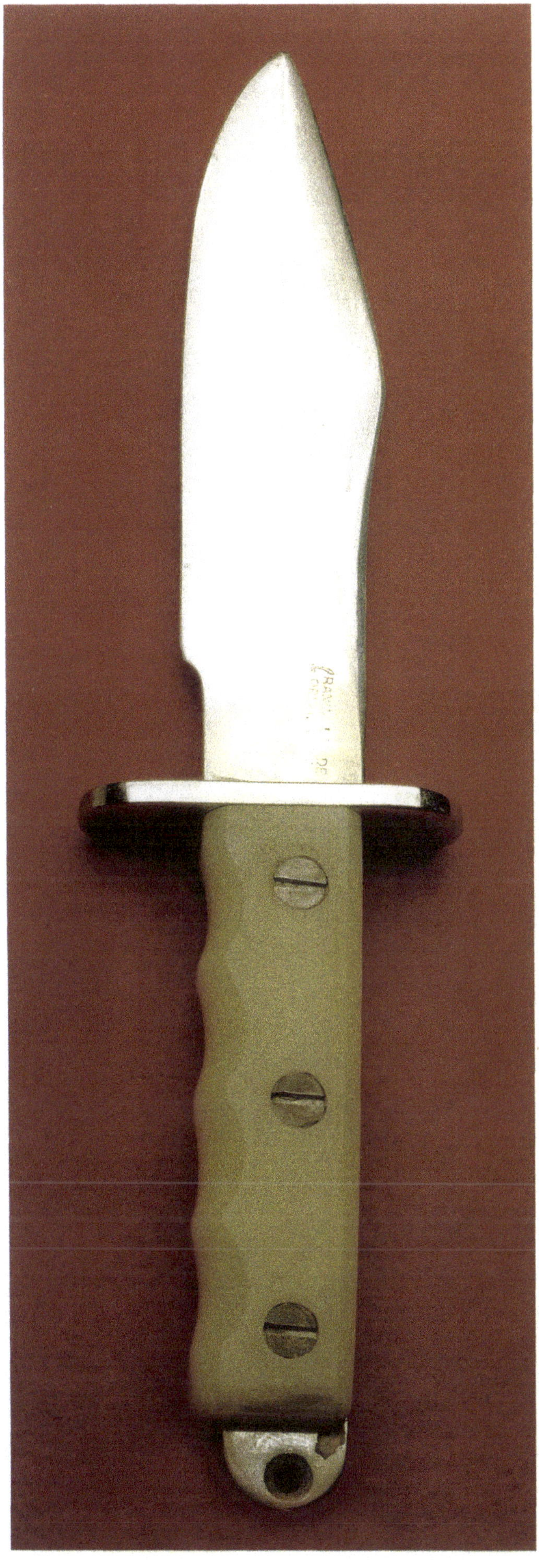

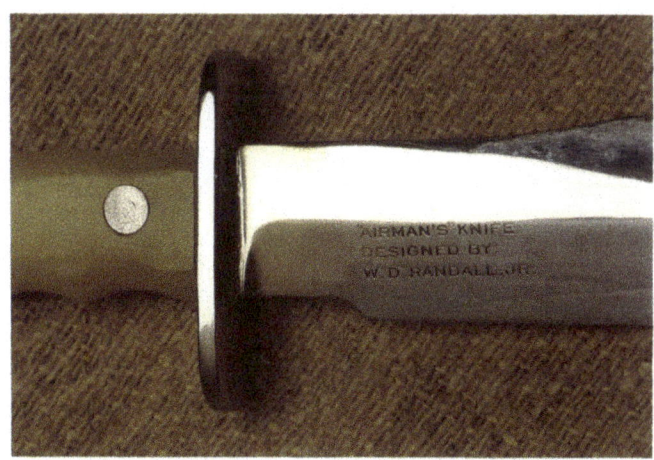

Model #15
5½" — Prototype knife

The blade on this prototype knife shows the upswept top line and sharpened clip that became synonymous with full tang knives during the early 1960s. The prominent hump would be retained on the Solingen blades, while Orlando gradually flattened the blade back. Viewing these Attack and Airman images serves to emphasize the power of their original design. Adapting a fighter-type blade to a full tang and flat guard greatly strengthened the model, while allowing for a more substantial blade without compromising the Model #1's proven style.

Astro Prototype with wire clip guard

This Astro configuration has been attributed to the requirement for designing safety features into the space knife and was intended to be a medical knife for the team doctor. The modification perceived the need to cover the sharpened clip of the blade for both storage and handling needs. The wire was designed to pivot back away from the blade or forward to provide a safe place for the forefinger during use. (The tape holds the wire in place and was not removed for the photograph.)

Note the brass guard on this example as well as the Astro cavity and handle wrap. The knife in this state serves as a three-dimensional functional design for this model and is interesting in and of itself.

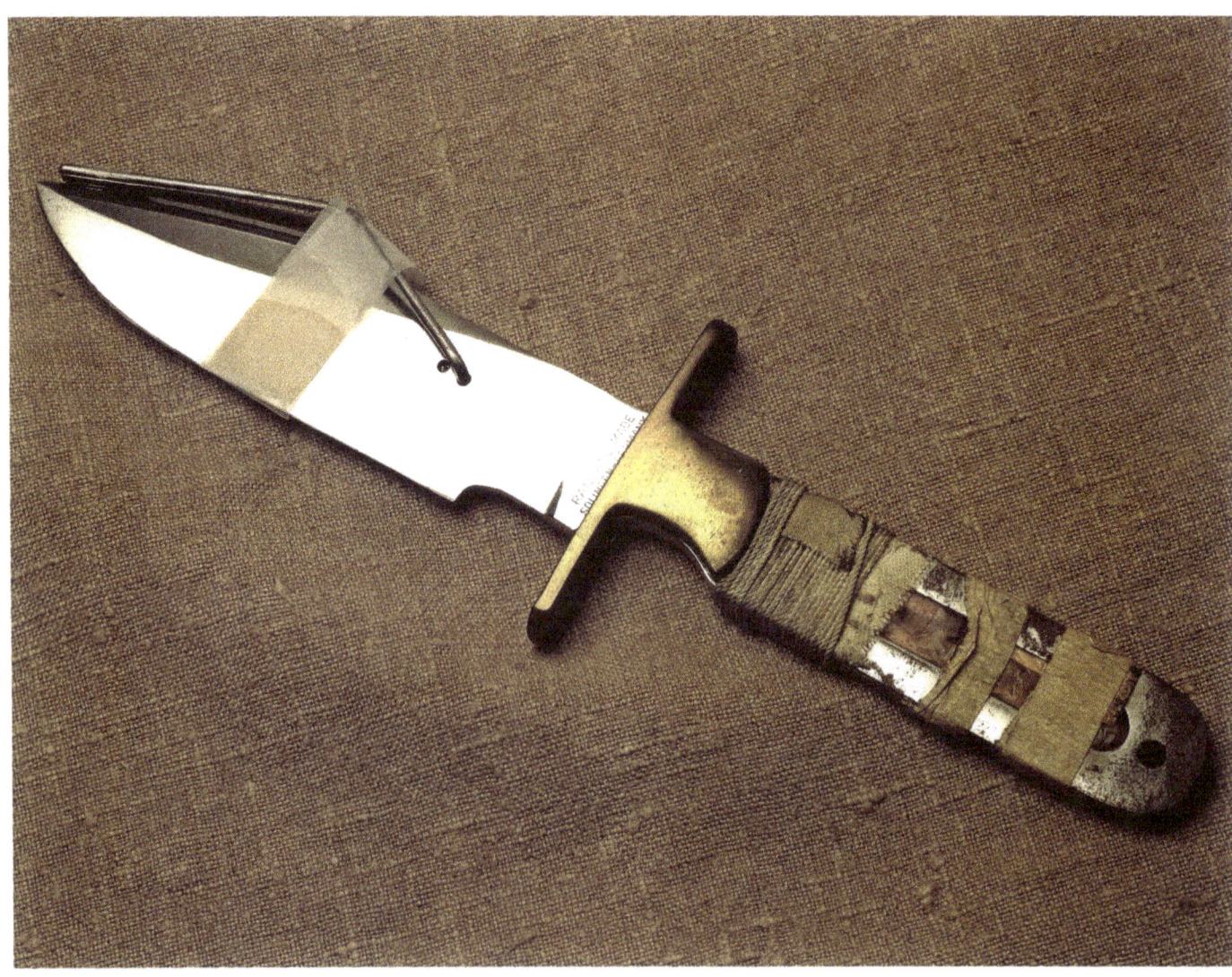

Astro with brass handles

Here is another example of the survival design; this one on the handle of a full tang Astro. The cavity in the tang is protected by brass handle slabs that rotate, pivoting on the pin at the guard. The thong is removed to allow for this procedure. Note the Model #15 grind on this early Astro experiment.

Astro Paperweight

This paperweight was made to commemorate the Astro, the first knife in space. They were offered in the Randall catalog or separate flyer and sold in the Shop. Approximately sixty-five were made.

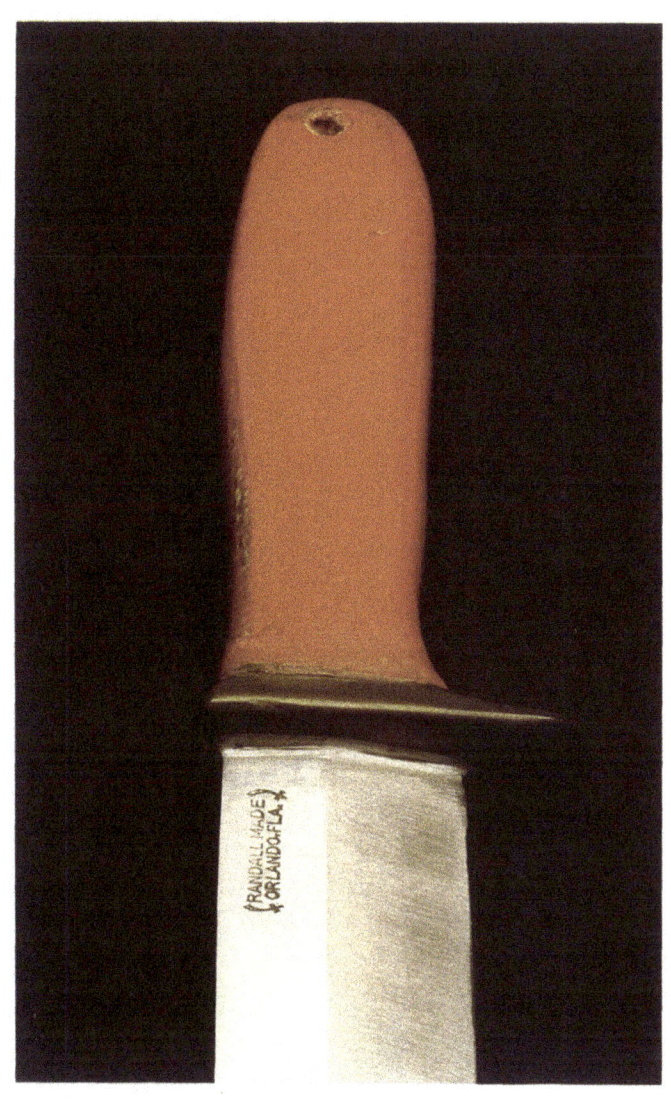

Diver with experimental handle material

This image depicts one of the many attempts to find a handle suitable for underwater use. The example photographed has a handle made from nylon webbing and some sort of compound. This knife was produced after the Diver model was established, probably during the early 1960s.

Original Prototype for the Commemorative Knife

The 50th Anniversary knife was designed along the lines of a Scagel-made knife. The example depicted here served as the original prototype and according to Gary, was one of several made, each being improved upon as they went along. The end result was this knife, the only one to be etched with Gary's name. Note the old-style handle and the spacer combination of leather, stag, fiber and metal. The finished knife is a beautiful piece of workmanship.

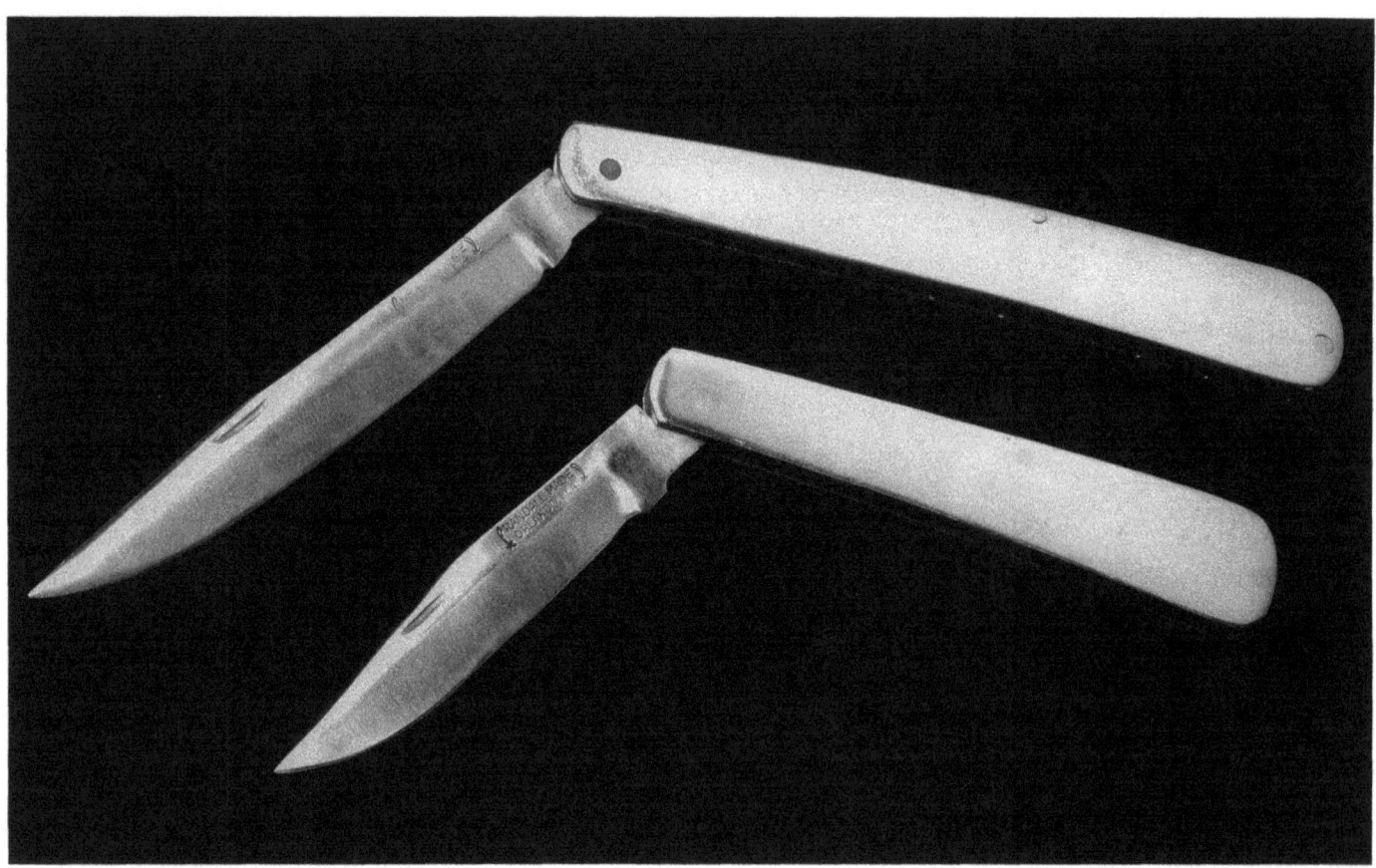

Randall Folders

The image here depicts two of the three folders credited to Bo Randall. They were made during the late 1940s with pinned aluminum handles. Interestingly enough, the top example had been lost and was located along Orange Avenue, retrieved from the gutter and returned to Bo. No such story accompanies the second of the two and the whereabouts of the third knife is unknown.

Stainless Steel Fish Knives

These knives are known to have been made beginning in late 1938 and represent Bo's earliest attempt to make a truly stainless underwater knife. An image of another appears in Randall Military Models, which is of some historic interest, but the two represented here predate it. Note the handmade trademark etching on the blade as well as the inscription and sail fish.

These knives were made from solid round stock, which allowed for the unique shaping of the handle as well as the integral thumb notch and guard.

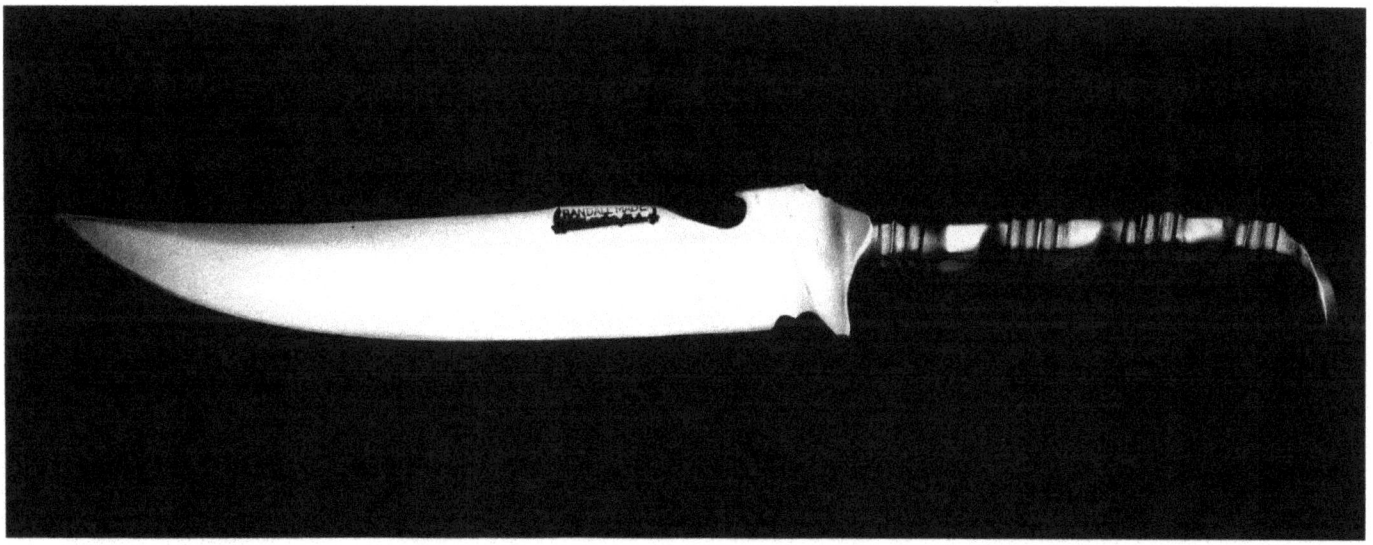

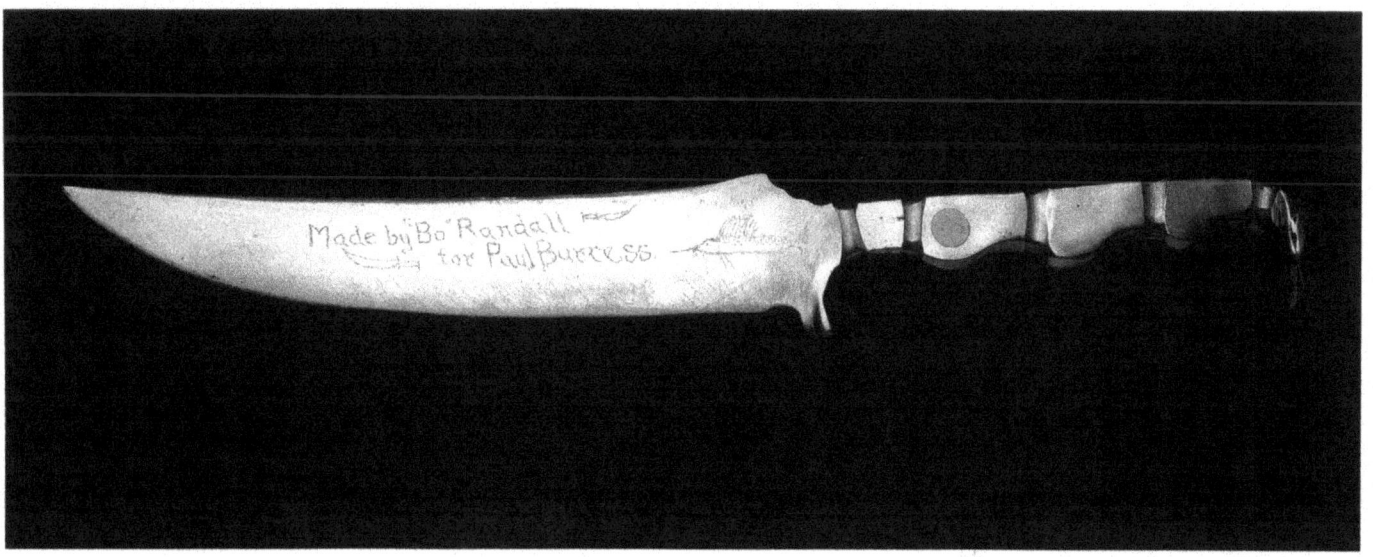

Spiked Thrower

This 8-ball was drilled and tapped and spikes were screwed into the ball. It was made to be held and gripped with the first two fingers and thumb and then thrown like a baseball. This "thrower" is reported to have been very effective and accurate, but not easily retrievable if several spikes struck a hard object. There is reportedly no sheath made for this device.

Engraved and Inlaid Hunter

This "Hunter", with 6-inch blade, is fully engraved with a carved inlaid handle, all done by Tom Leschorn. It was W.D. Randall's personal knife and was presented to Bo in commemoration of the 50th anniversary of Randall Made Knives.

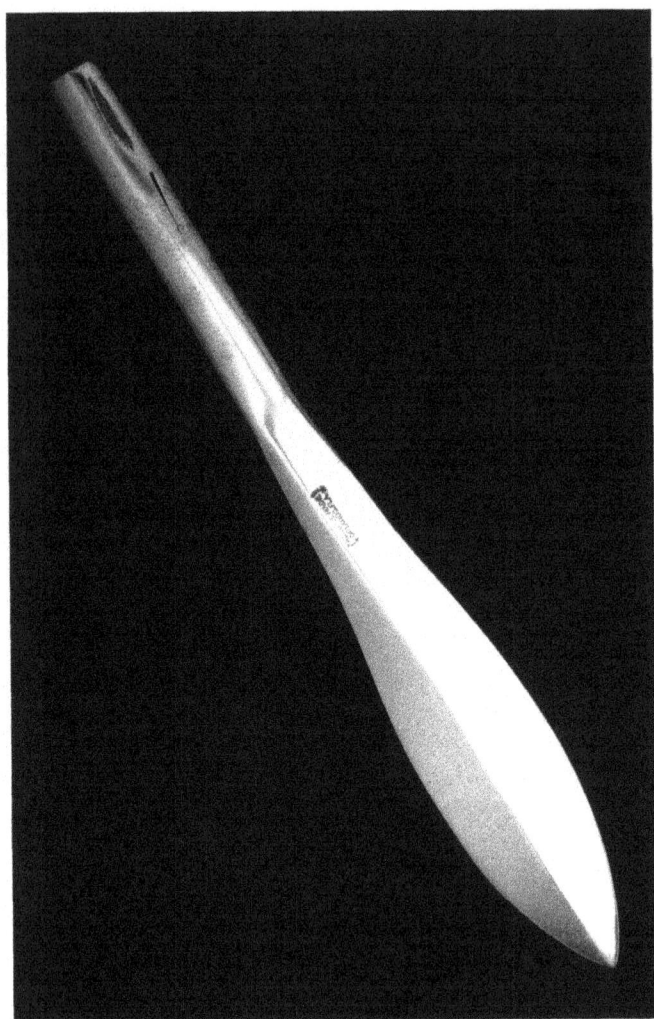 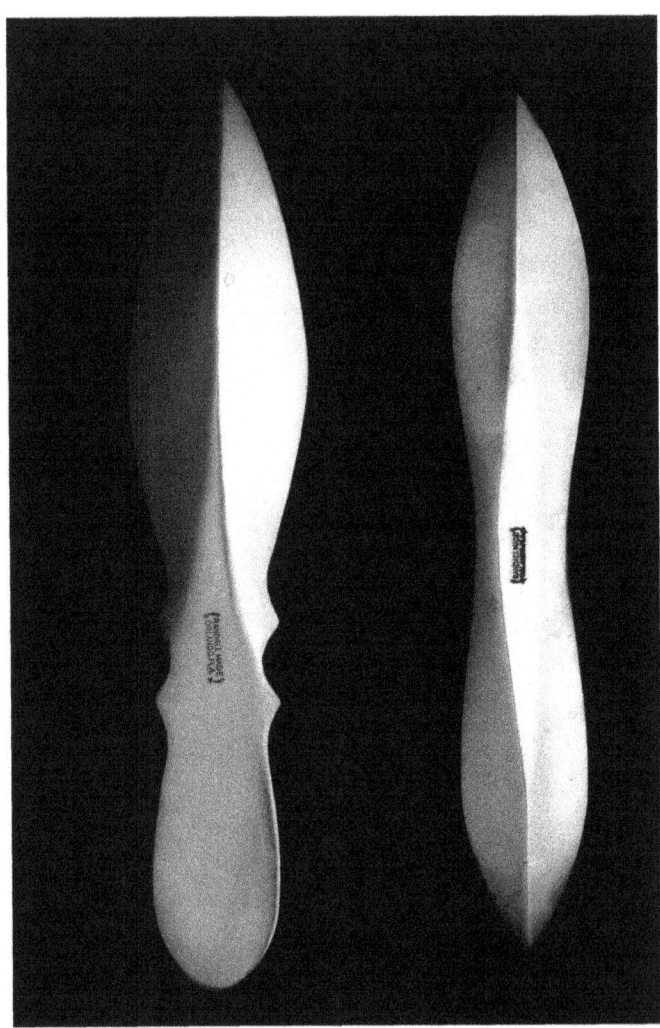

Pro-Throwers

The following images depict the development of the Randall "pro-thrower" and represent some of the styles built on the way to the final catalog offering. The example with the round steel handle may have been one of the first designs and was repeated in leather. Throwers were made with broad blades to facilitate a hand-hold. Bo favored these knives and threw them, so he knew a little about their design and construction. Gripping techniques were based on the number of revolutions during travel to the target and the distance dictated the type of hand-hold and therefore the handle design.

The illustrated pair shows the left thrower grooved for finger placement on the edges, while the rounded butt would rest in the palm of the thrower's hand. The knife on the right would require the thrower to grip the knife along the edge, but permitted more leeway in revolutions en route to the target.

The leather-handled example allowed the thrower to get a traditional grip. This shape shows little contour and the narrow blade compliments the handle. Note the brass bolster, small stamp and spacer arrangement. Circa 1950s.

That this experiment had neared completion is reflected in the dimensions of the Flat thrower, which closely approximates the ultimately adopted version introduced in the catalog. Like many of the RMK models, there is an experimental "trial" period traceable from the concept design phase right up to the catalog offering.

Gary Randall has pointed out to the author that "many knives were made to try out designs . . . some changes were incorporated, some not" and went on to say that during the early days, pre 1970, finished knives of unusual design were sold and circulated in the field.

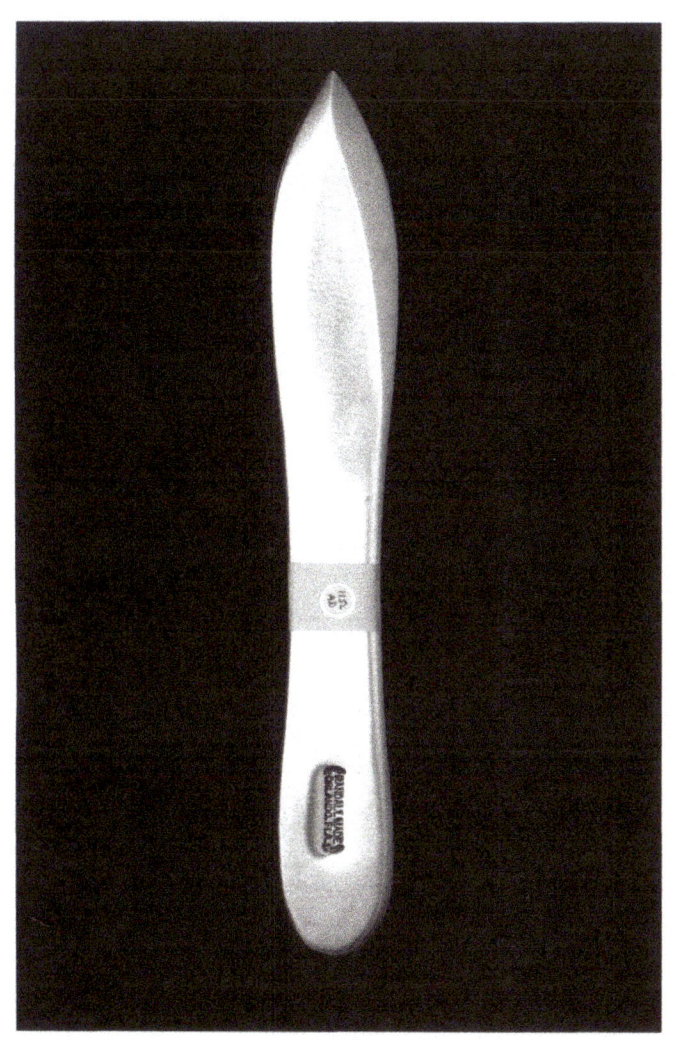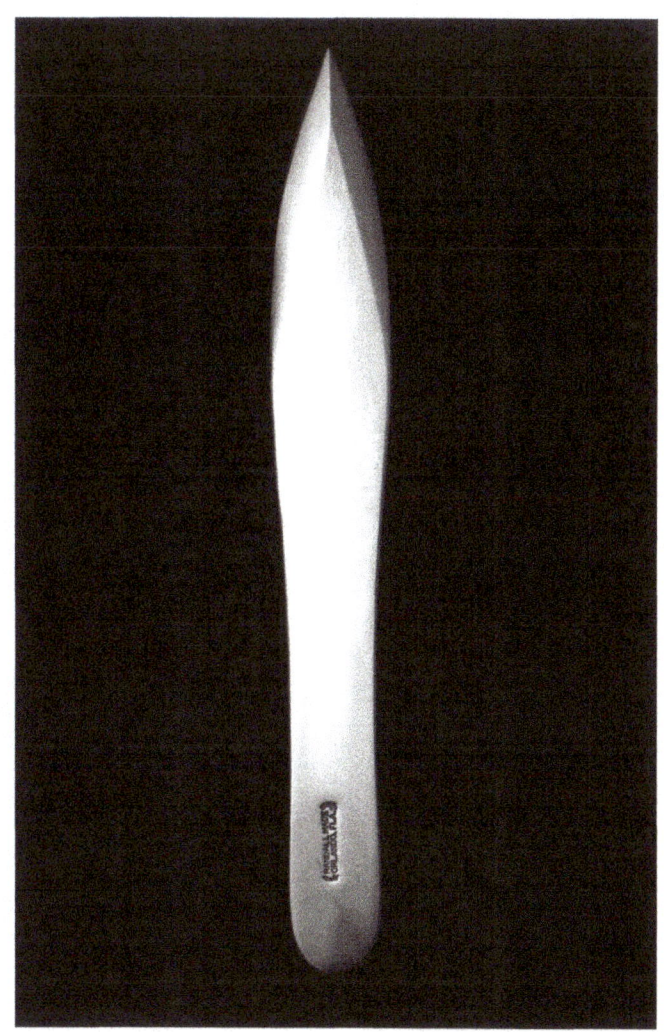

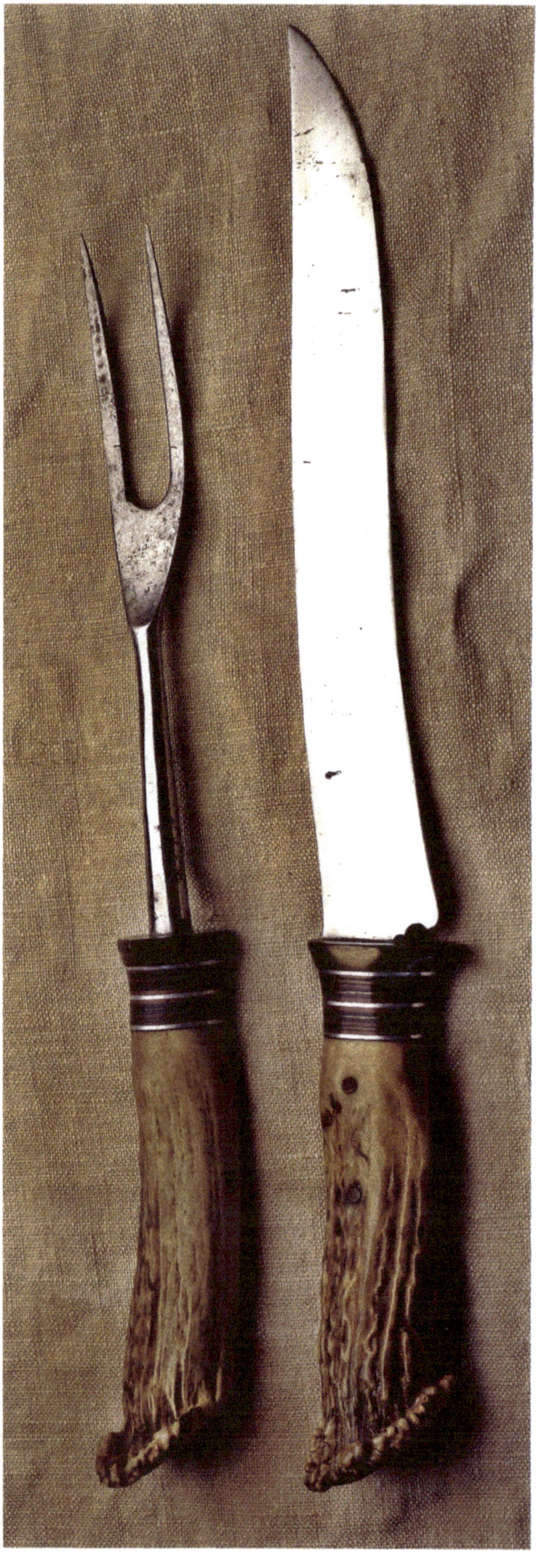

Early Carving Set

This carving set appears to be of 1940s vintage, and represents one of the two styles of Henckle carver blades known to have been used at that time. The Stag is very early and double-pinned. Spacers are metal and the half-guard is smoothly contoured. Note the Spanish Notch on the blade. The fork is without the stand, which was a subsequent design change.

Early Stag Hunter

Depicted here is a late 1930s Hunter-type showing discernable Scagle influence. The blade is six inches long with Randall's typical upswept tip. This same blade type was to carry over into the early 1940s in one of Bo's fighter designs referred to as the Commando. Note the hand-etched "trademark". The guard on this knife appears to be integral with the handle, which is pinned stag. The spacers are wood, fiber, brass and aluminum.

Sickle-shaped Skinner

As with many of the knives in the museum, the motive for producing various examples was experimentation. This radically shaped knife blade was made at a time during the 1960s when "skinners" had no apparent limits in upsweep; although I suspect that it may have reached it in this example.

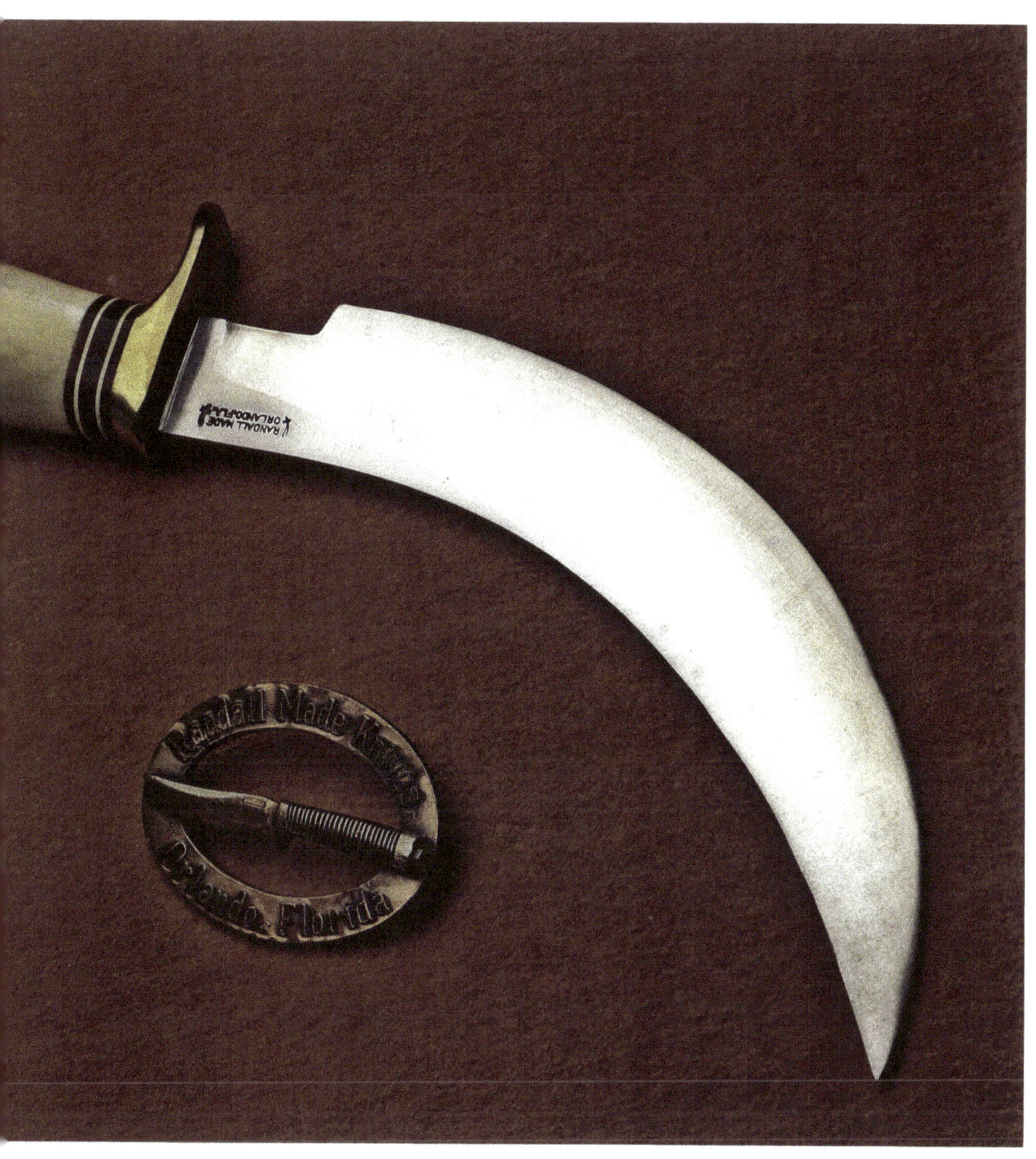

Ivory Bowie set – 1950s

The motion picture "The Iron Mistress" was released sometime during 1952 and the story has been recounted that Bo made a likeness to satisfy customer demand. The Smithsonian, as it has come to be called, is the "heavy" Bowie depicted in this pair. In Gary's memory, these knives represent the first two Bowies made. Gary's initials are etched into the escutcheon plates on the handles. The Smithsonian has a brass back and the "Toothpick" represents the other type blade, wheeled by an adversary in the bowie knife fight filmed in the movie.

Handwork abounds in this historical pairing; at the collars, guard and butt cap. The blades are chromed and therefore bright and the lugged hilts are braised.

Gemini Bowie Ax

Following the success of the Model #17 "Astro", other knife designs were experimented with seeking suitability for space (astronaut) requirements. This is one of those knives. Qualifying as a machete, this 8-inch blade full tang knife, featured a deep belly and steeply angled clip. The long ricasso added strength and the hilt is a brass half-guard. The handle material is micarta, bolted to the tang.

This is a unique blade design, probably based on Astronaut specifications and actually the smaller of two designs known to exist.

Full Tang 8" Bolo

Somewhere along the line the M1917 medical bolo made an impact on either a customer or Bo himself. This knife appears to represent RMK replication of that early style hospital or medical bolo manufactured in the tens of thousands during WWI. An overall likeness between the two is where the similarities end however. This knife has a handsome blade design and exhibits many notable improvements over the original. It carries with it a 1960s flat guard in brass and a filled screw hole, black rippled micarta handle with finger grooves.

8" Bowie, circa 1950

At RMK the "innovations" never seemed to end. Although Mr. Randall did not, as wishfully believed, make all of the knives in the shop even in the 1940s, his hand is seen in the design features of many of the 1950s and 1960s models. This one incorporates a finger groove handle and fighter hilt, as well as a Sheffield Bowie style clip with a full belly on the blade. Note that there is no nut at the butt cap, which is drilled for a thong hole.

Ary Tendon Cutter

The angles on this knife are a bit different, which dictated the positioning of the image. The heavy blade makes a downturn at the point, without losing much blade width. Designed by a customer to compliment his style of knife fighting, the Ary tendon cutter name is descriptive even if the style is a bit unorthodox. The handle is a commando, swelled-center type and the spacers 3 medium-thick, 2 thin. Reportedly it was made during the late 1950s.

Kukri

A familiar design on the Indian continent, this knife style was made famous by the Gurghas, a warlike people who carried and used them extensively and with deadly efficiency. This example may have been a customer request, or one of Bo's experiments, but it is now archived and fills a place in the Randall Museum. This chrome-bladed creation has many upgrades, including a walnut handle, butt cap and hand-forged ground and polished blade.

Bear Bowie

The "Bear" was late arriving on the Bowie scene and it didn't really depict a 19th century traditional side knife, as the others did, but rather a customer's impression of a knife that you might kill a bear with. A real bear that is. If not realistic, it is quite handsome and represents some interesting grind lines and "furniture". Initially made during 1964, this example with forward-curved hilt has a low "s" on the ricasso. The rosewood handle is swelled in the center with an eagle of silver inlay. The miniature "Bear", which is the work of Randall employee Walter Grigg, is part of the museum collection as well.

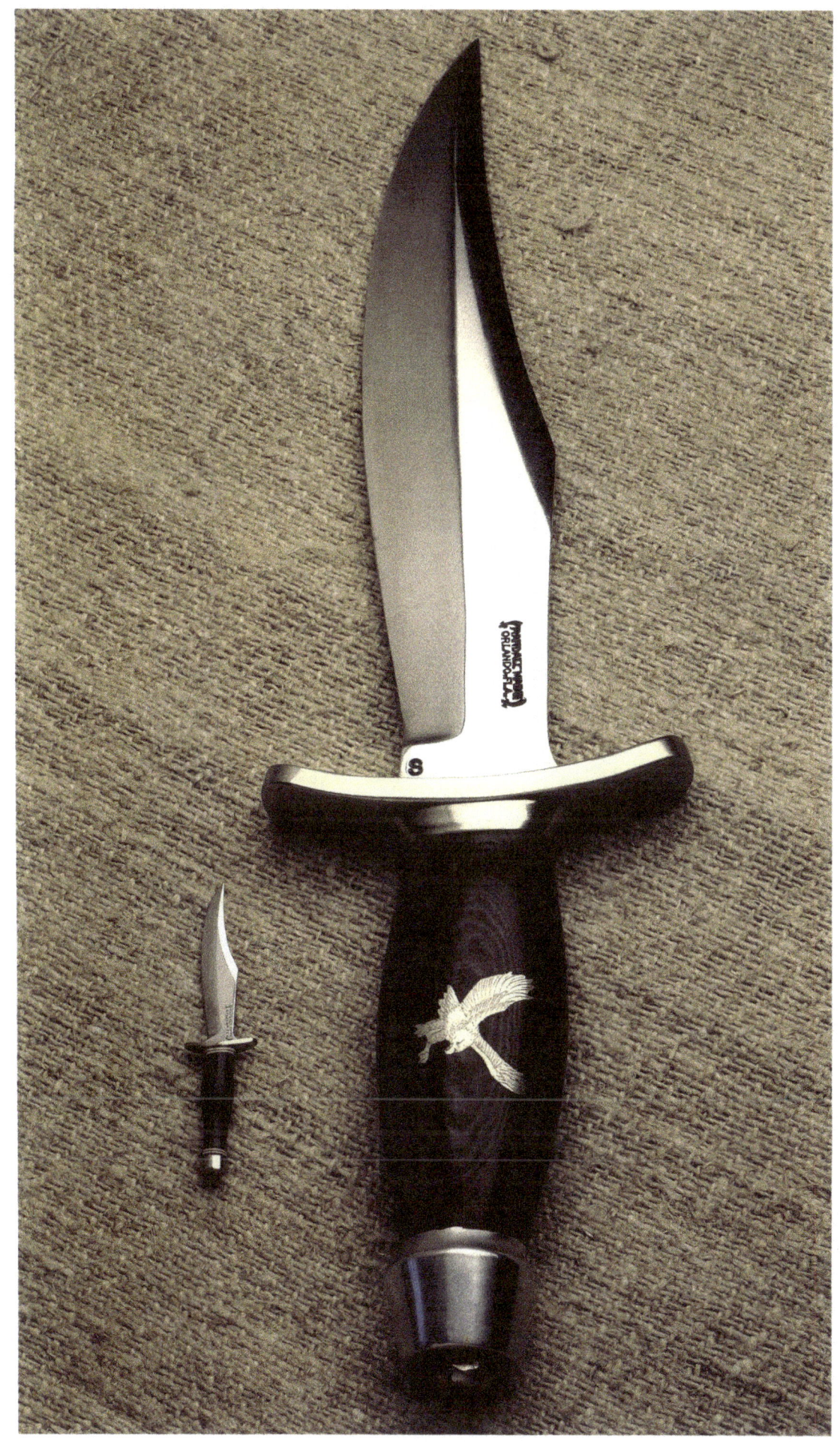

Section II:
"Experimental" Randall Knife Collection

The original owner of this collection, Finis Westbrook, was an avid knife collector during the 1960s. After his passing in 2003, his knives were cataloged by his son. They included makers G.W Stone, Bone, Clyde Fischer, Gil Hibben, Pete Heath, a large assortment of early case pocketknives and a dozen or so knives made by Bo Randall.

My interest led to the Randalls, fifteen in all, twelve of which are experimental; seven etched that way on the blade, along with the date, 1965. I purchased the collection. There was no available information indicating any direct connection between the collector and Bo. All twelve of these knives, whether blade-etched "Experimental, 1965" or not, had their origin in that period and were kept together for these past four decades, while concealing some very unique characteristics. The continuity of this grouping serves to support and reinforce the significance of their shared characteristics.

At that moment I was left to speculate as to what provided the catalyst for the innovations represented in these various knives. Although Bo produced a special customer designed knife from time to time, these accumulated examples, all designed and produced about the same time, required another explanation. Later, during the compilation of material for this book, including the photography and subsequent research connected with the Randall Museum images, the experimental "root" of the question became much clearer.

Eleven of these knives all share a common characteristic: the use of narrow or reduced stock, (3/16" or 1/8"), rather than 1/4", which is standard on most catalog items.

In addition to the above, each knife includes at least one of the following unusual features: use of experimental handle material, reduced full tang(s), a cut-down tang on a full tang-only model, full tang construction on "special stiletto" grinds, introduction of a new design years before catalog, and shop handling of non-Randall manufactured blades. In the case of eight, there is a Randall shop etching on the reverse side of the blade, Experimental, 1965. Further, all but three of the "experimental" blades bear the Randall logo. The three exceptions were handled by Randall Made Knives with standard spacers and standard handle material.

All of the knives are accompanied by mid-1960s, customized to fit, mint JRB, Randall Logo sheaths in like-new condition, just like the knives.

The remaining two knives documented here were with the collection and although "used" and predating the origin of the remainder, nonetheless share "rare" characteristics. These two are described as: 1) an early 1950s Bolo with 12-inch blade and Moore sheath, and 2) a nineteenth century frontier hunting style design with 8-inch blade, accompanied by an unmarked sheath with a brown button, circa 1950s.

The sole record referencing these knives was found contained in a letterhead envelope marked "Important Randall Knife Papers" and accompanies the collection. The envelope contained two note pages, handwritten and dated 1/1/67, listing the knives and bearing a brief description of each. The collection is presented in the order that they appear in the original notes. The handle labels exhibited were affixed by the previous owner and appear to have been in place since he acquired the knives. The detailed descriptions accompanying the images serve as text and are the author's.

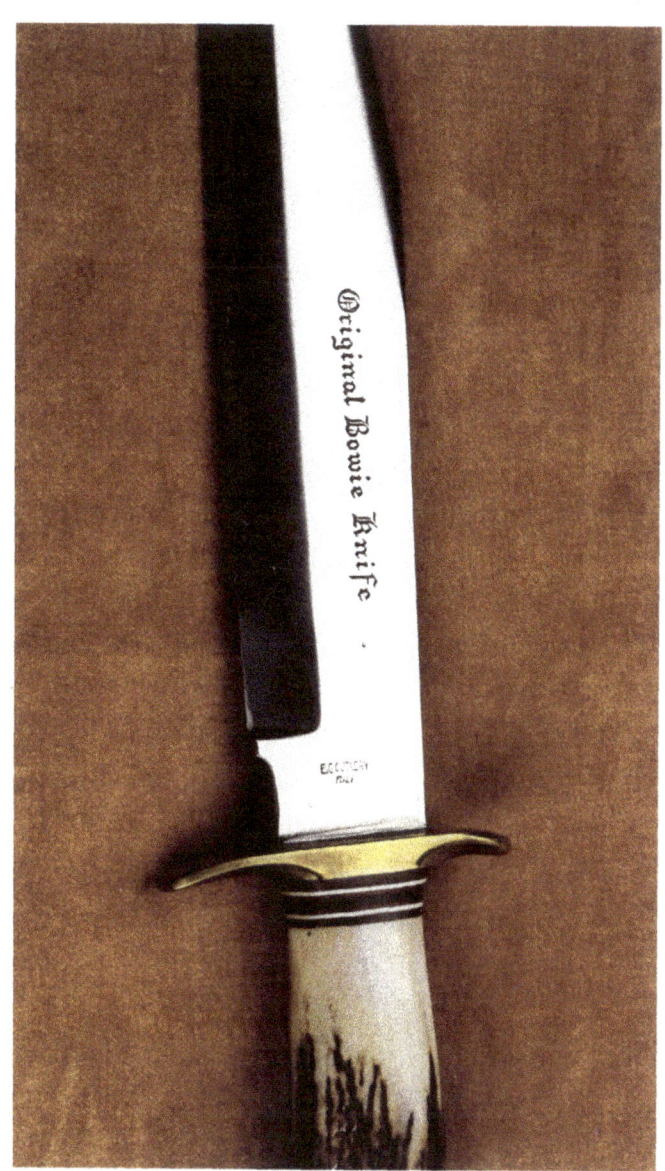

Bowie knife with 8-inch blade, etched "ORIGINAL BOWIE KNIFE" with a ricasso stamp, EIG Cutlery Italy

The reverse side is etched Experimental, 1965 by Randall. This knife was also handled by Randall, with the standard configuration of brass guard and stag handle with 7-spacer stack.

Accompanying note states "Blade was too soft to consider," which implies that this information must have come from Randall and explains why more weren't made. The knife is in mint unused condition.

IXL Randall-Wostenholm Bowie

This is the one item in the collection that has reference and Gaddis documents its genesis in detail. There appears to have been eighty-four 10-inch blades stamped with the Sheffield England maker's mark, which were handled by RMK, but were never illustrated in the Randall catalog. (Coincidentally, this is also the timeframe (1965) when the rest of these knives were made.) Condition is unused with some storage marks on the blade. Note the IXL stamp.

Model #12-6 Stag English Bowie

It is marked on the ricasso, WADE & BUTCHER, SHEFFIELD ENGLAND, the company that made the blade, which appears to be ground from $3/16"$ stock. This is a hunter design, not completely unlike the small Wosterholm hunter that was offered at the same time. The handle, half-guard, and the spacers are standard Randall. The sheath is a JRB marked 1-6. (This is the same manner in which the small 6-inch Wostenholm Bowie was sheathed.)

Model #14 with standard 7½" Solingen blade

Numbers 4 & 5 are listed together on the note pages. The first is a Model #14 with standard 7 ½" Solingen blade. It has the Randall logo on the obverse side and is blade-etched with Experimental, 1965 on the reverse. Special design features include narrow contoured red fiber handle slabs, held in place by three screws or bolts, lined with brass and filed flat. Handle length is five inches. Tang was reduced to $3/16$" under the handle slabs. The knife is guard-less. The result is an "Attack" model with reduced profile and "flat" dimensions. Weight was reduced from the standard model at 15 ½ oz to 11 ½ oz. A JRB sheath with handle keeper (guard-less knife), without a stone pocket and without model or blade markings, accompanies the knife. Condition on both the knife and sheath is mint/unused. The handles are not drilled for a wrist thong.

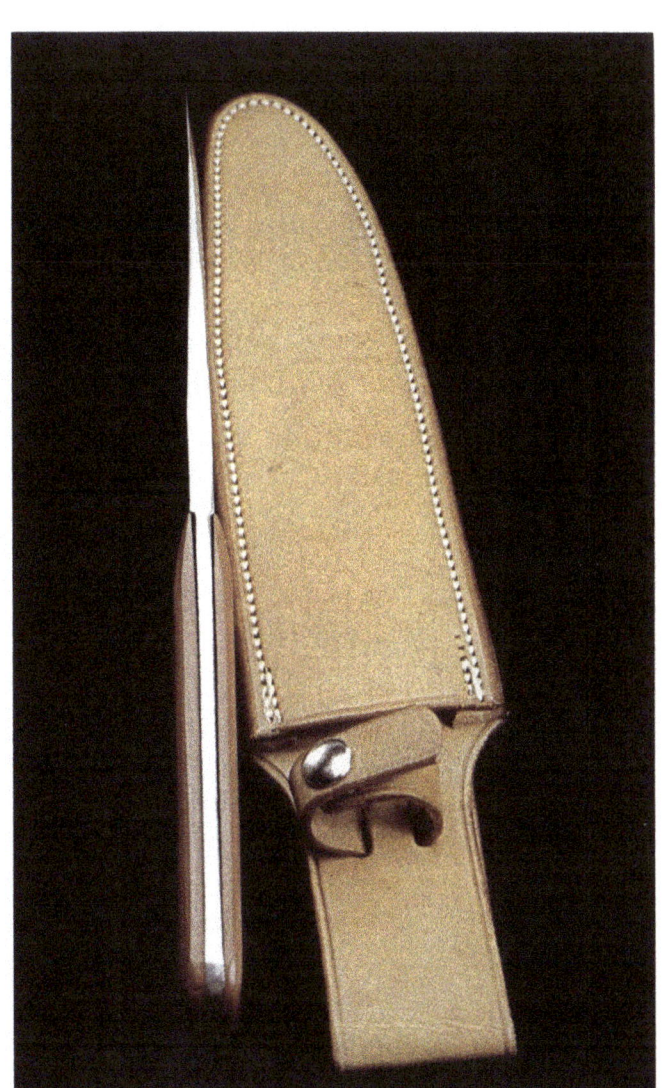

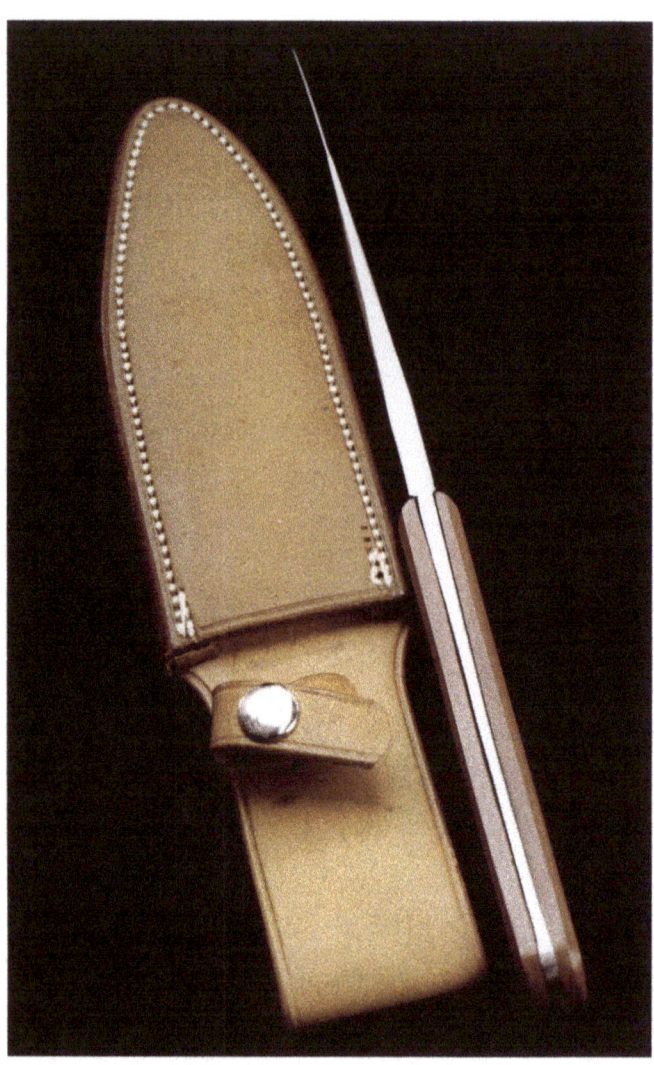

Model #15 with 5 3/4" Solingen blade

The accompanying number 5 is a Model #15 with 5¾" Solingen blade. The Randall logo appears etched on the obverse side and the reverse side is shop-etched Experimental, 1965; the stock is ¼". The tang is reduced where it joins the handle to ³/₁₆" and tapered to ⅛" at the end. It measures 4 ⅝ inches in length. The handle slabs are made of red fiber and are bolted in place with three steel screws with brass liners. Both ends are filed flush with the handle. The sheath is a mint/unused JRB without stone pocket and without markings. It is a custom fit, as is the preceding knife sheath combination. These knives have every appearance of being a pair of special design.

Knives of this type were offered under SOLINGEN BLADES Another Adaptation and illustrated on page 9 of the Catalog (sixteenth printing, 1965), using standard Solingen blades with "... .a handle made of ¼-inch vulcanized fiber, attached to the tang with rivets" and were offered at a reduced price. This pair, marked Experimental, 1965, obviously served as the design prototype for this modification. By the seventeenth printing (1966), this special model was withdrawn. As a catalog item, it remains a rare example of a Randall made knife totally forgotten until these "first design" knives were discovered in the Westbrook Collection, thirty-eight years later. The appearance of the pair serves to close the loop on the project as well as shedding light on the genesis of these unique Randall design modifications.

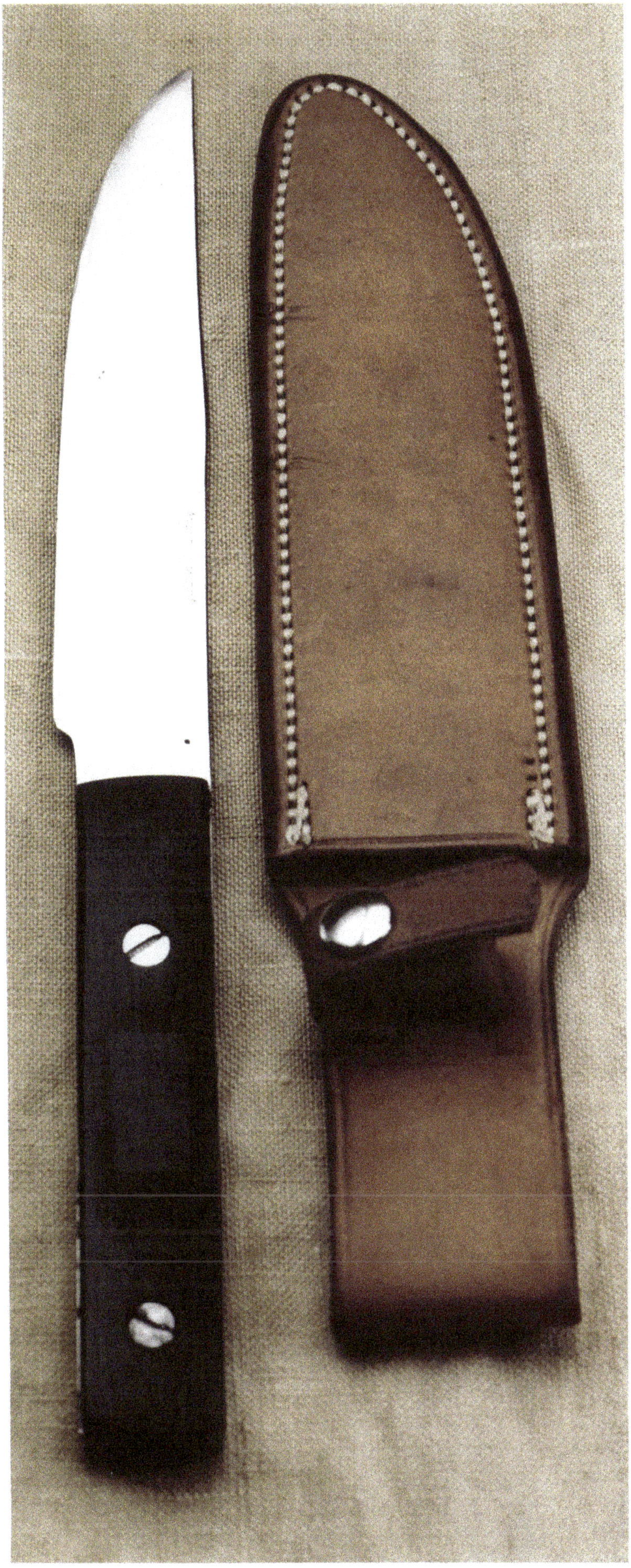

Referenced Experimental 1965

Referenced Experimental 1965 and so etched, this is a kitchen knife of forged carbon steel and 6 $^1/_2$" blade length. The stock is $^1/_{16}$" and the full tang is handled in black micarta slabs, held in place by two steel screws and liners. The forging process is very clearly recognizable on the blade. The knife is accompanied by a JRB sheath without stone pocket similar to numbers 4 and 5. Both knife and sheath are in mint/unused condition.

1-8¹/₄" Fighter

This knife is referenced in the notes as "1-8¹/₄" Fighter of ³/₁₆ stock; (1 of 2 made)" and actually measures ¹/₈" thick. Design features include a narrow blade, deep choil and short guard (2 ³/₈" long) as well as reduced overall dimensions. Blade depth at the choil is 1". Weight is 8½ oz, two ounces less than the standard configuration with this blade length. The handle shows the same proportional reduction in width as the blade. Spacers at the guard are typical for the period, but reversed in color: blue/white/red/white/blue. Two medium blues and a thin white at the butt cap. The blade is stamped with the Randall logo and in its original polish. The sheath is a JRB with model and blade marking. Both are in mint/unused condition.

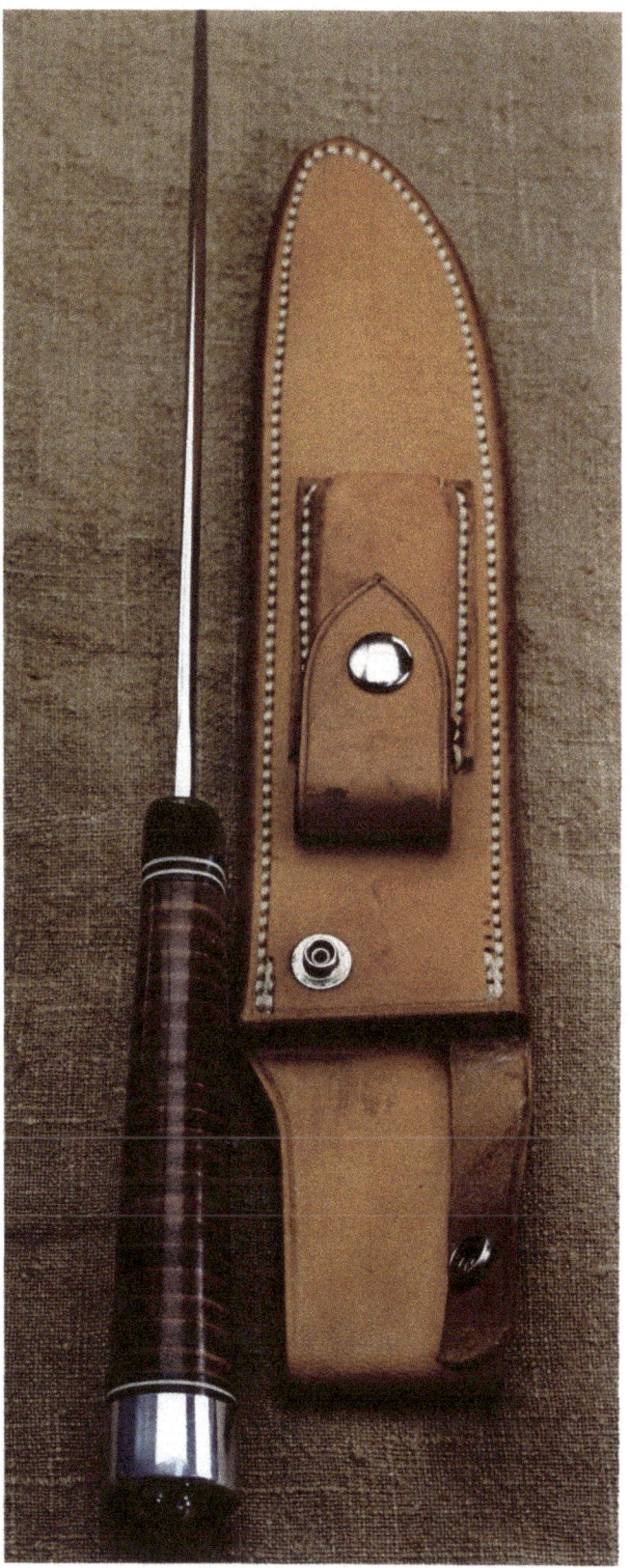

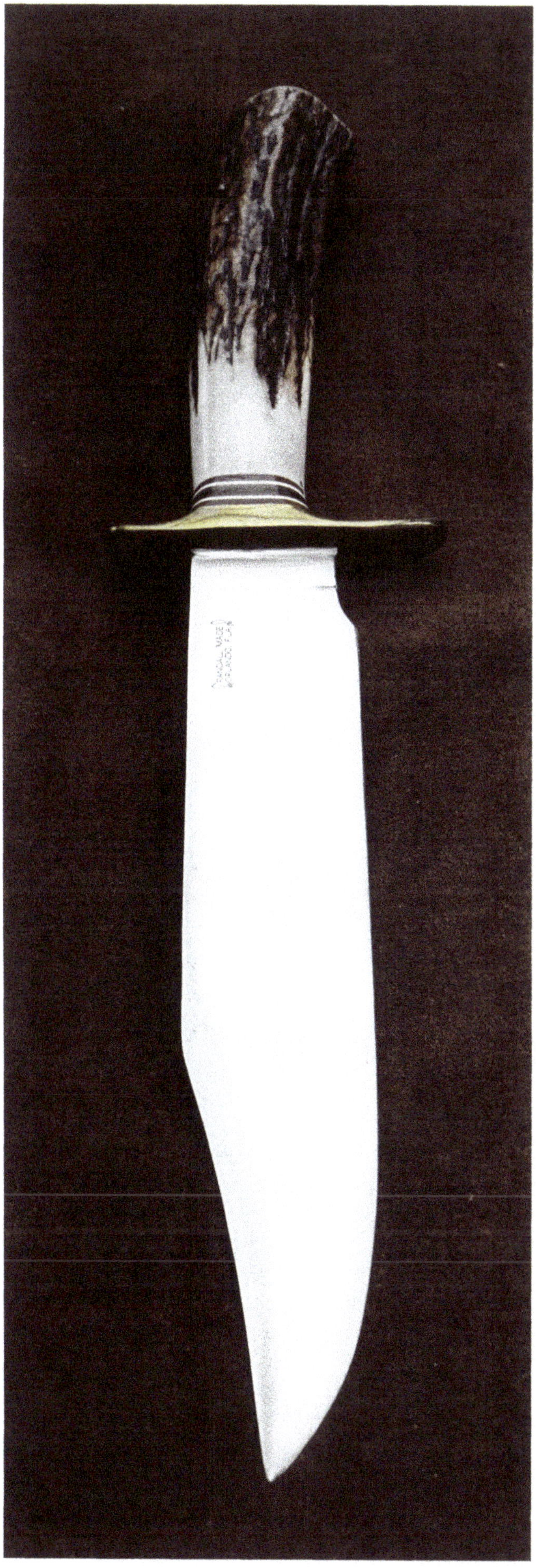

#12-9 Sportsman's Bowie

The referenced notes identify this knife as "#12-9 Spts. Bowie with thin blade, stag handle 1 of 2." The knife appears to be standard in all other respects. The blade is logo-etched, with a brass guard, 7-spacer configuration and stag handle without cap. The blade thickness measures $1/8$" but was probably made from $3/16$" stock. The weight is 13 oz., a three-ounce reduction from standard configuration. This is a handsome knife and it is accompanied by a JRB sheath with model and blade markings both in mint/unused condition.

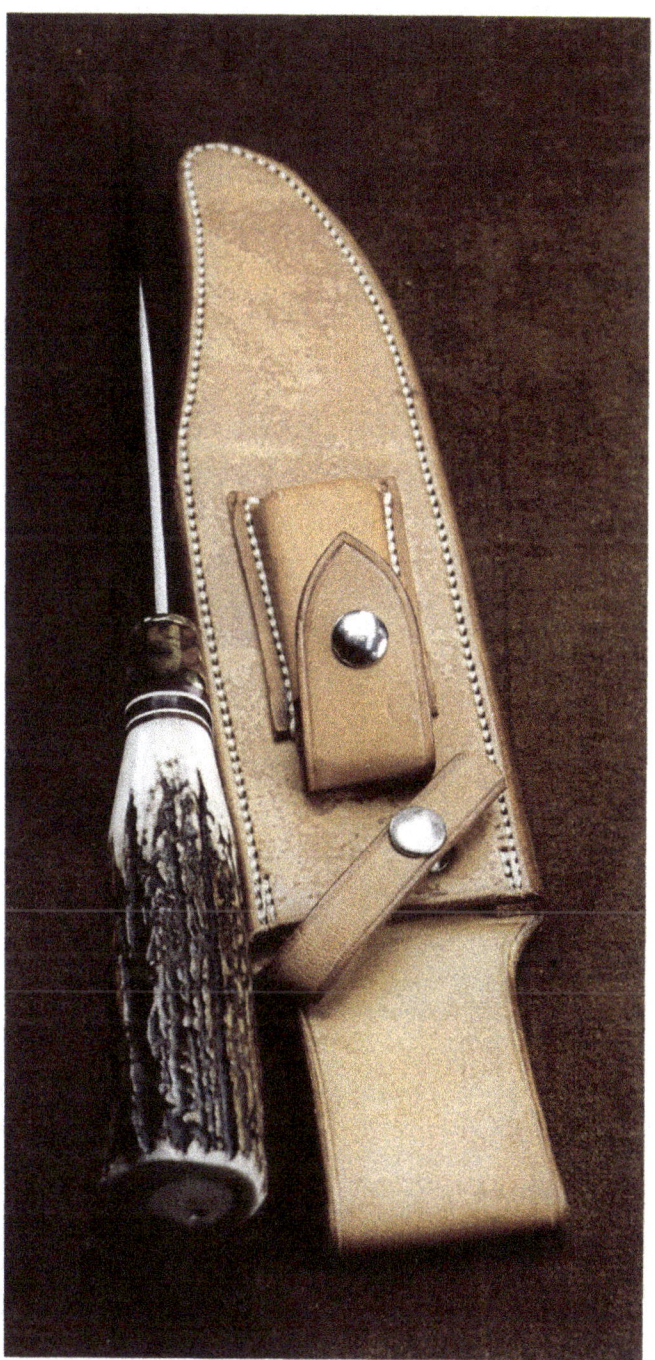

#18-7 1/2" NSH – Stag handle

"1 of 2 made – unusual" is how the entry appears in the collector's notes. Design features include an Orlando blade, saw-teeth, nickel silver half-guard, thumb notches, 7-spacer arrangement and stag handle. The blade is from standard ¼" stock and is carbon steel. Condition is mint/unused and the knife is accompanied by its sheath, a riveted split-back Johnson with leather ties. This configuration was recalled by Gary Randall as having been made during this time period.

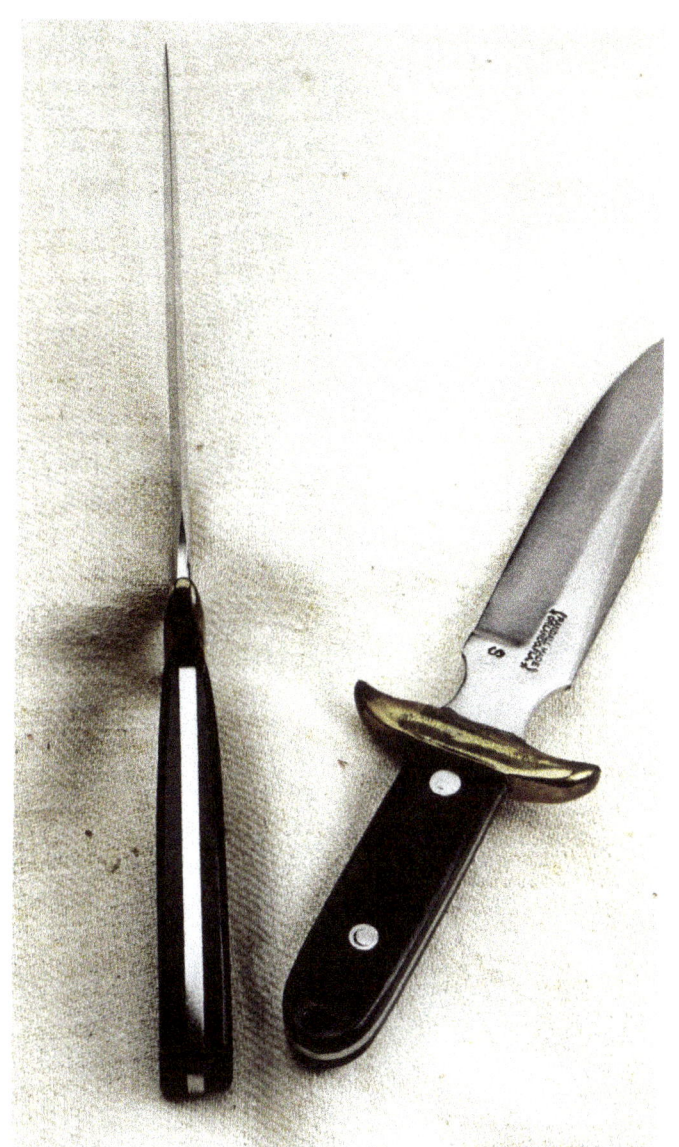

Special Stiletto

The notation for #s 10 & 11 reads "Special Stiletto, SS Both "Ex". These are special knives and the most significant and impressive of the collection. The first has a 6" Orlando blade with a stiletto grind, choils, marked with a low "s" and forged from 3/16" stock. The reverse side is etched Experimental, 1965. The construction is full tang. The guard is uniquely shaped brass, forward curved and silver soldered. The handle measures 4" in length with brown micarta slabs affixed by two screws concealed under the handles of both knives is an "astro" cavity in the full tang. The JRB sheath exhibits a "custom" contouring at the throat, in order to accommodate the shape of the hilt. Note the wrist thong hole drilled through the handle and tang.

Special Stiletto

The second knife, also of full tang construction, has a modified stiletto design with ricasso, but was obviously "designed to be the Model #1 fighter-type" of this unique pair. The grind is flat and the blade is stamped with a low "s". The reverse side has Experimental, 1965 etched above the median. There are double choils of slightly unequal dimensions due to the ricasso. The top of the 6 $1/4$" blade is sharpened almost four inches, but an overall stiletto look is retained. The stock is narrow and measures $1/8$", therefore appearing to be wafer thin. This knife has the same shaped brass hilt, which is conducive to moving the gripping fingers forward of the guard to rest in the choils and could be used as a push dagger. The black micarta handle is quite short, measuring 3 $1/2$" and it is bolted in place. These knives give every appearance of being designed as a pair and compliment each other; notwithstanding some subtle differences. They represent a very convincing stealth-concealment design for penetration and extraction with a flat profile for carry.

A knife of similar design, with the same blade grind in 6" length, is displayed in the Randall Museum. That knife, also of full-tang construction, has not been handled and the fully exposed tang reveals a Model #17 Astro-like cavity between the two bolt holes. The silver soldered brass guard is identical, but with reduced upper quillon (half-guard) and the exhibited blade does not show the low "s" found on the special stiletto(s) featured here.

JRB sheaths with stone pockets accompany both knives, but without model or blade markings. Additionally, both exhibit identical contouring at the throat in order to fit the unusual shape of the guard when the knives are seated. The pair represents a most eye-appealing, innovative and practical stealth fighter design. The condition of both knives and sheaths is mint/unused.

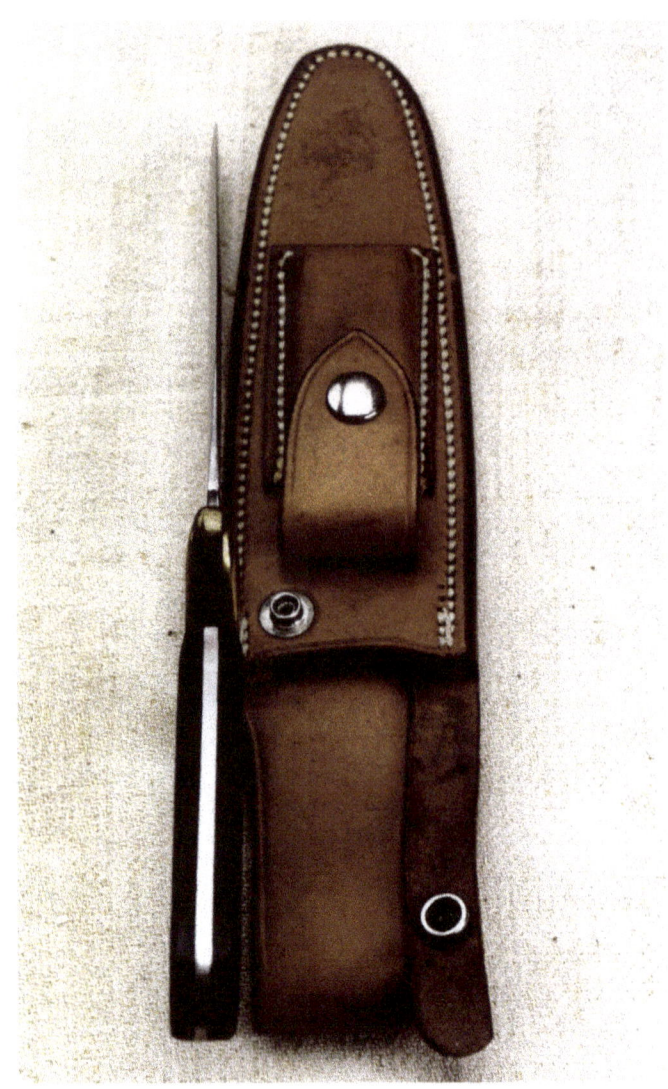

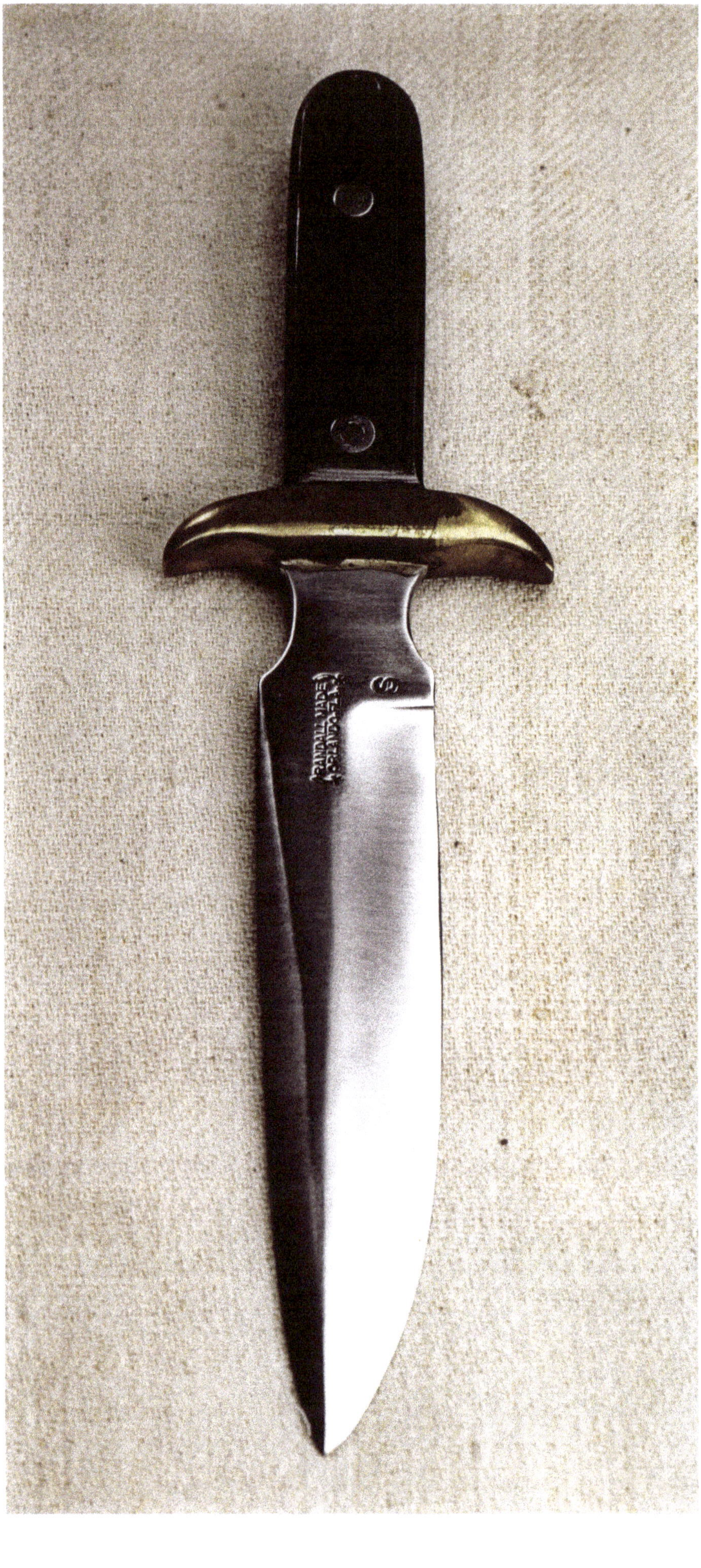

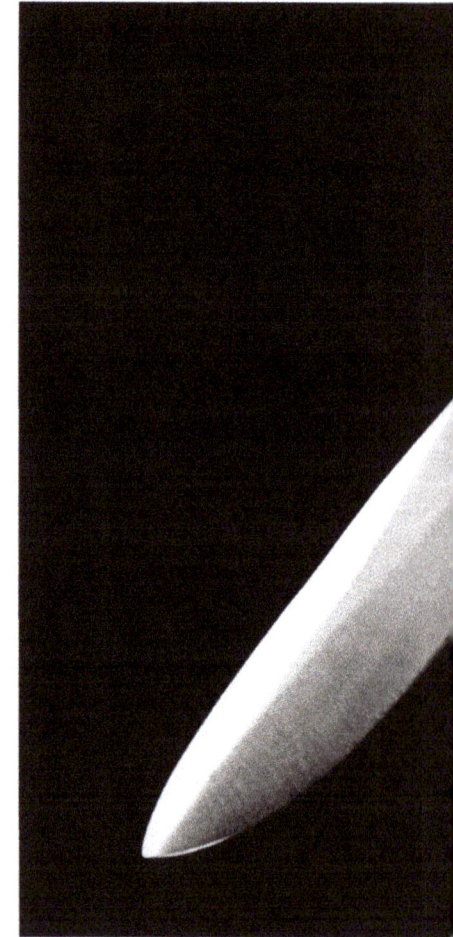

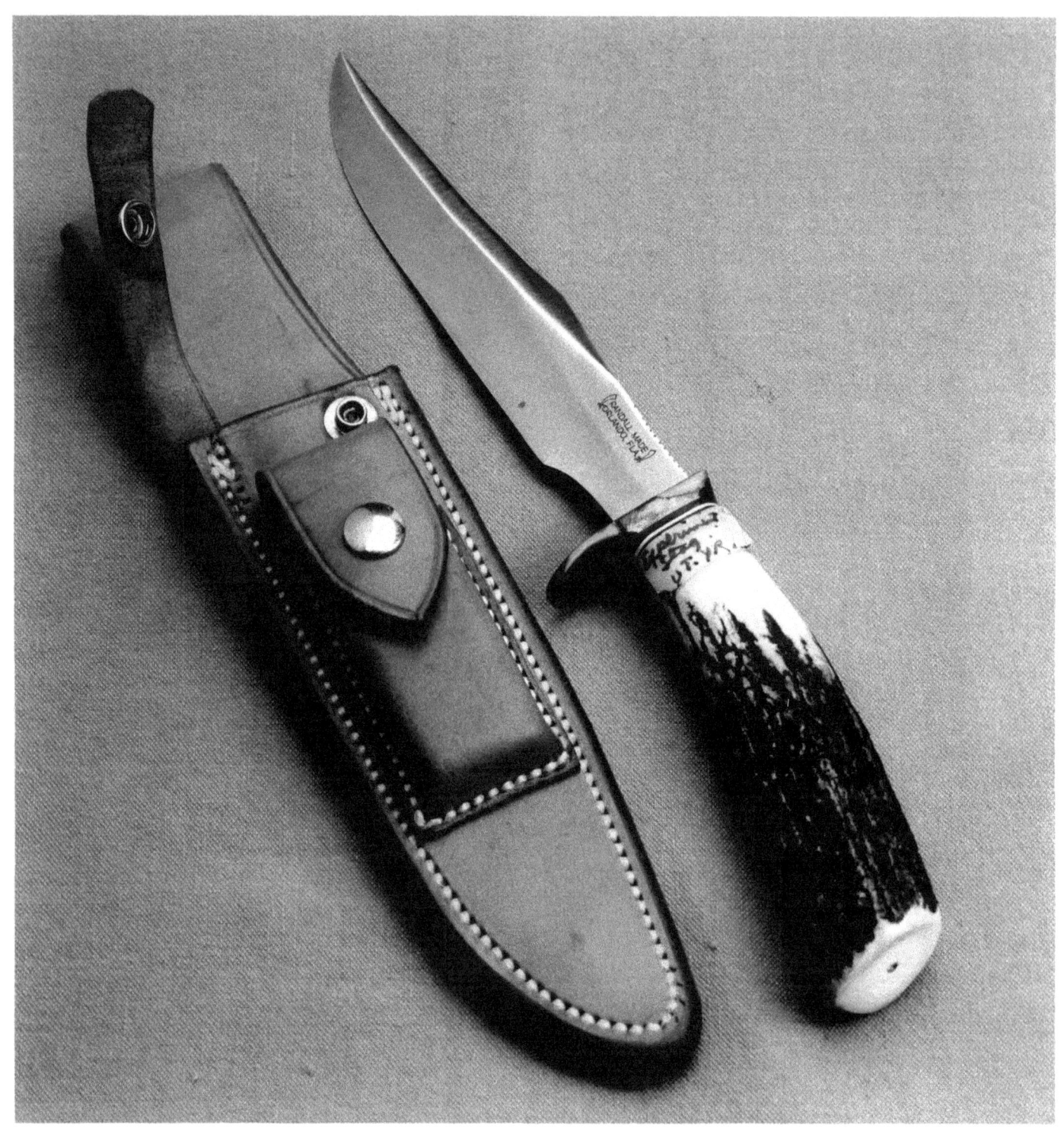

Model 12-6 "Little Bear Type"

A Model 12-6 "Little Bear type" of ³/₁₆" stock and carrying the Experimental, 1965 etching on the reverse side. The handle is stag; spacers are standard, as is the reduced brass guard. This is two full years before this model was introduced in the catalog. The sheath is a JRB with no model or blade markings. Both are in mint/unused condition. This knife is referenced in the notes as "Special Stag Bowie Type" and "very unusual" and "fine", "1965".

Note: All stones are two-tone gray, unused and marked with mint lettering "Combination Crystolon Made in U.S. of A."

Special Stag

A "Special Stag" notation identifies the fighter-type knife depicted here and serves as a distinction from the "Little Bear" type previously illustrated. The blade back has been sharpened for more then two inches and angles from the logo-stamped ricasso down to the tip. The stock is thin and the reverse side of the knife is stamped with the same Experimental, 1965 marking. It is a blade grind not previously encountered by the author. The sheath is marked on the back "3-6". (Courtesy of Bobby Westbrook.)

The two aforementioned knives not referenced as "experimental," but belonging to the collection and having unusual and rare characteristics follow as #s 14 and 15.

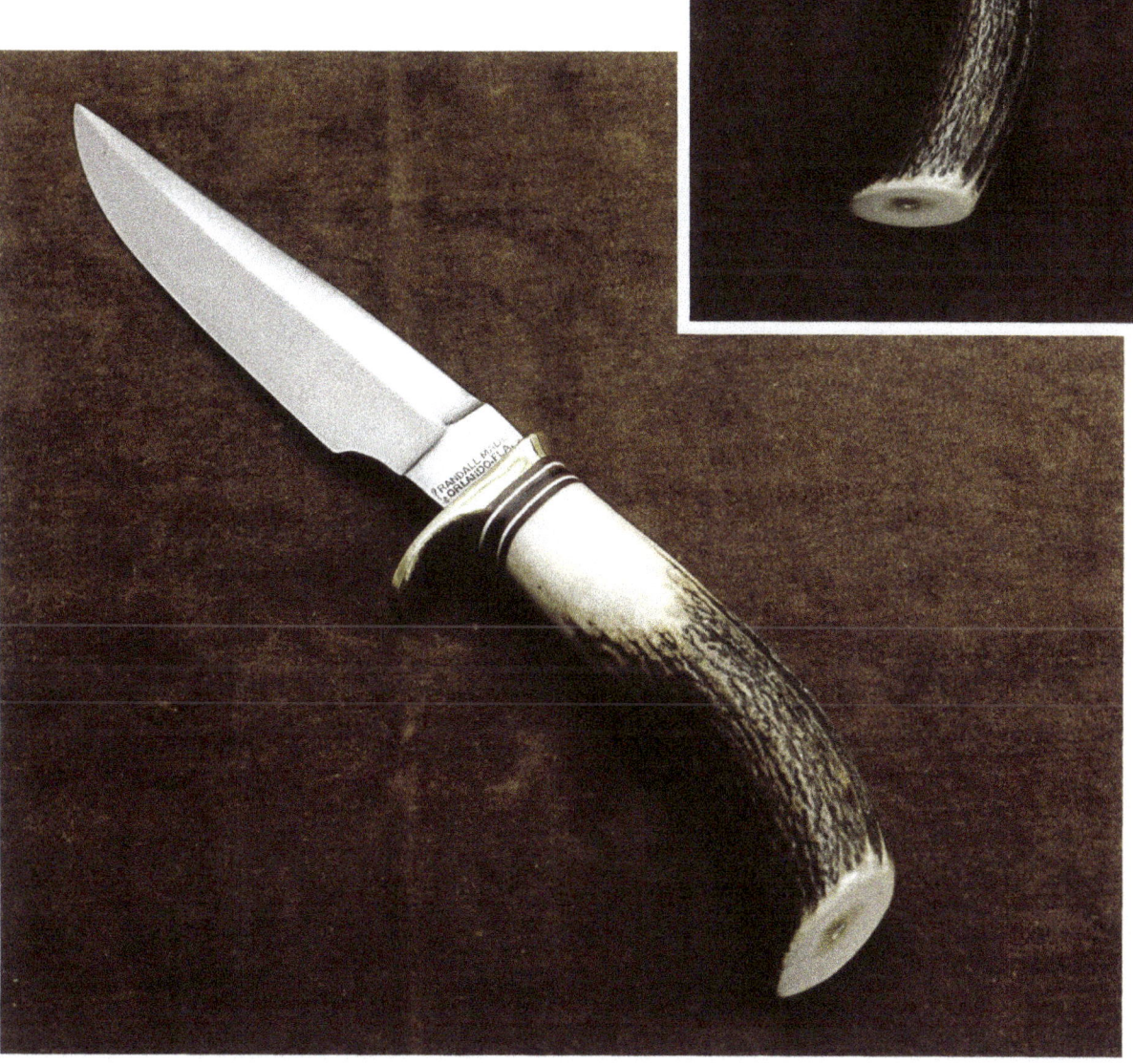

Randall Bolo

Randall Bolo, with 12" blade, leather handle and medium-thick spacers. This knife appears to be of early 1950s vintage. Note the handle washers that are uneven in width. It is not a catalog item. The author has photographed one other and it was depicted in Randall Knives in Wartime, WWII section, on pages 46-47. The latter was probably of 1943 production. This knife is of a later design, with a more generous bolo-like blade that is full with a very deep stamp and looks as if it had a light cleaning at the Shop. It is accompanied by its Moore sheath, which has an interesting etching on the front that reads in part, "The Alaskan" and "the finest blade that ever slit a throat." Perhaps that is why the blade was cleaned.

Hunting design

Nineteenth century "type" Hunting design. This appears to be a Randall variation of an early style large hunting or "bush" knife. The blade measures 8" and looks to have been ground from $3/8$" stock, but measures $1/16$" narrower than Smithsonian Bowie blades. The stamp is full and deep and the blade has been polished. The guard is rectangular and squared off on the ends (no lugs). The handle is concave, unusual in leather washer configuration and has a rounded brass butt cap and hex nut. Spacers are all medium thick. The knife is probably of early 1950s vintage and is accompanied by a quality period sheath without markings.

Conclusion

The preservation of this collection intact and in its original state, (over the intervening forty years) shows the care and interest taken in their ownership. It also indicates that something beyond a "casual" interaction existed between the owner, or another, and Bo Randall; most certainly a collaboration. The reference to "1 of 2" or "1 of 2 made" in the original notes, as in #s 7, 8 and 9 may imply that Bo made another of those specific knives. This has yet to be determined, but with the exception of the "Special stiletto" pair, numbers 10 and 11, no others were found by the author in the Randall Museum. With the exception of the "Little Bear" type and the fiber-handled Solingen blades offered in the sixteenth printing, few of the experimental features were ever introduced on a standard model offered in the catalog and notwithstanding their specific design innovations, further attests to their uniqueness.

The middle 1960s, and 1965 in particular, was apparently a time when Bo Randall was interested in experimenting with new designs. The Astro, in brown micarta with the etching of that date on the blade, is just another example and though not a part of the "collection", is being depicted (in another section) for that reason. The date, if not the knife itself, has some significance.

This material was prepared by the owner of this collection, Robert E. Hunt, and is presented in this volume along with numerous other examples of the innovative and experimental tradition of RMK. It reveals many things, including the high level of collector interest in these knives as long ago as 1965.

Most importantly, it exhibits a dozen interesting and innovative "unique" designs, with representative examples from the Randall Made line: Fighters, Bowies, full-tang attack-survival knives and hunters. Discovered individually, each or any one would serve to excite the imagination. Collectively, they represent a milestone in the history of Randall Made Knives.

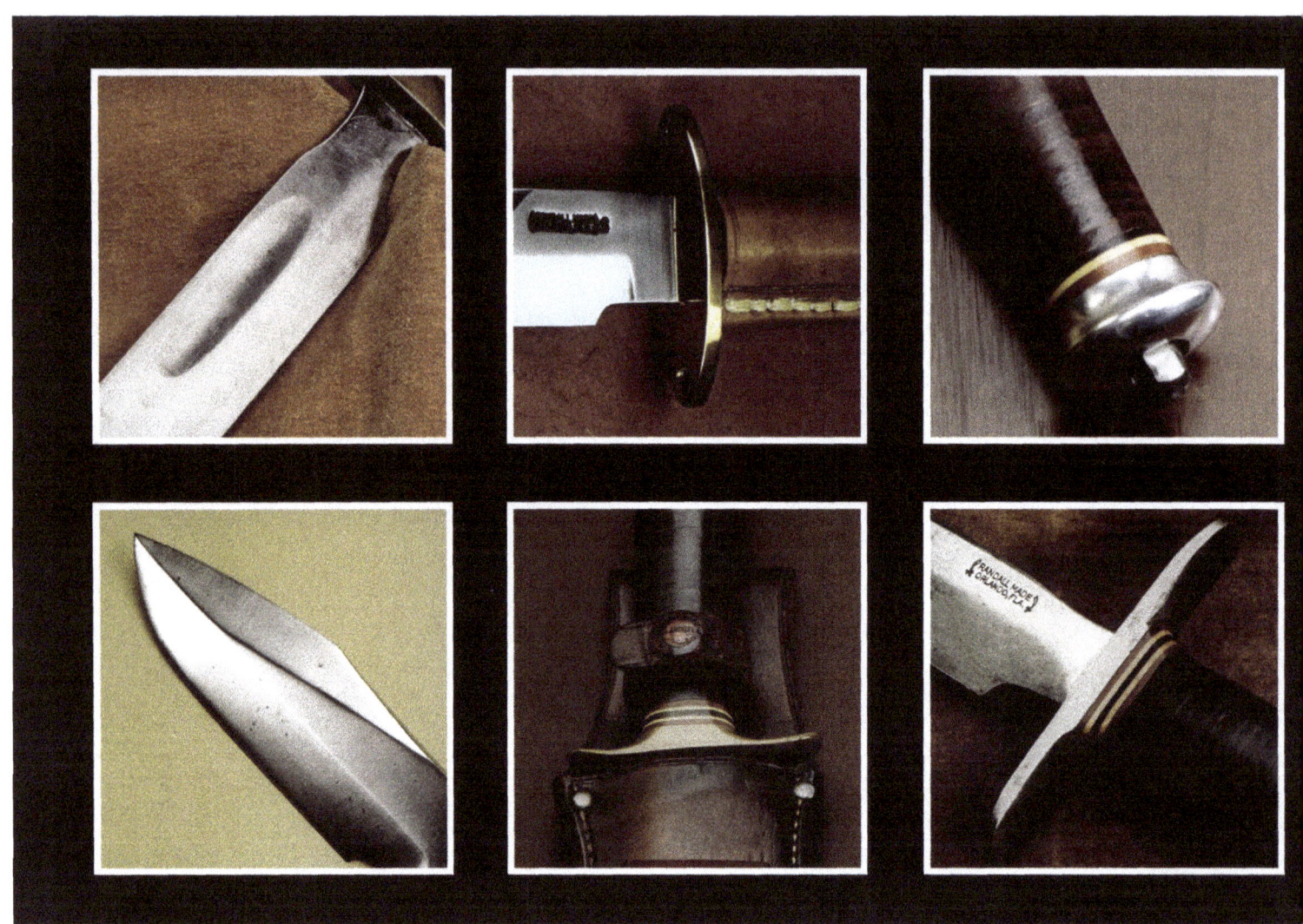

Section III:
Rare and Unique Knives

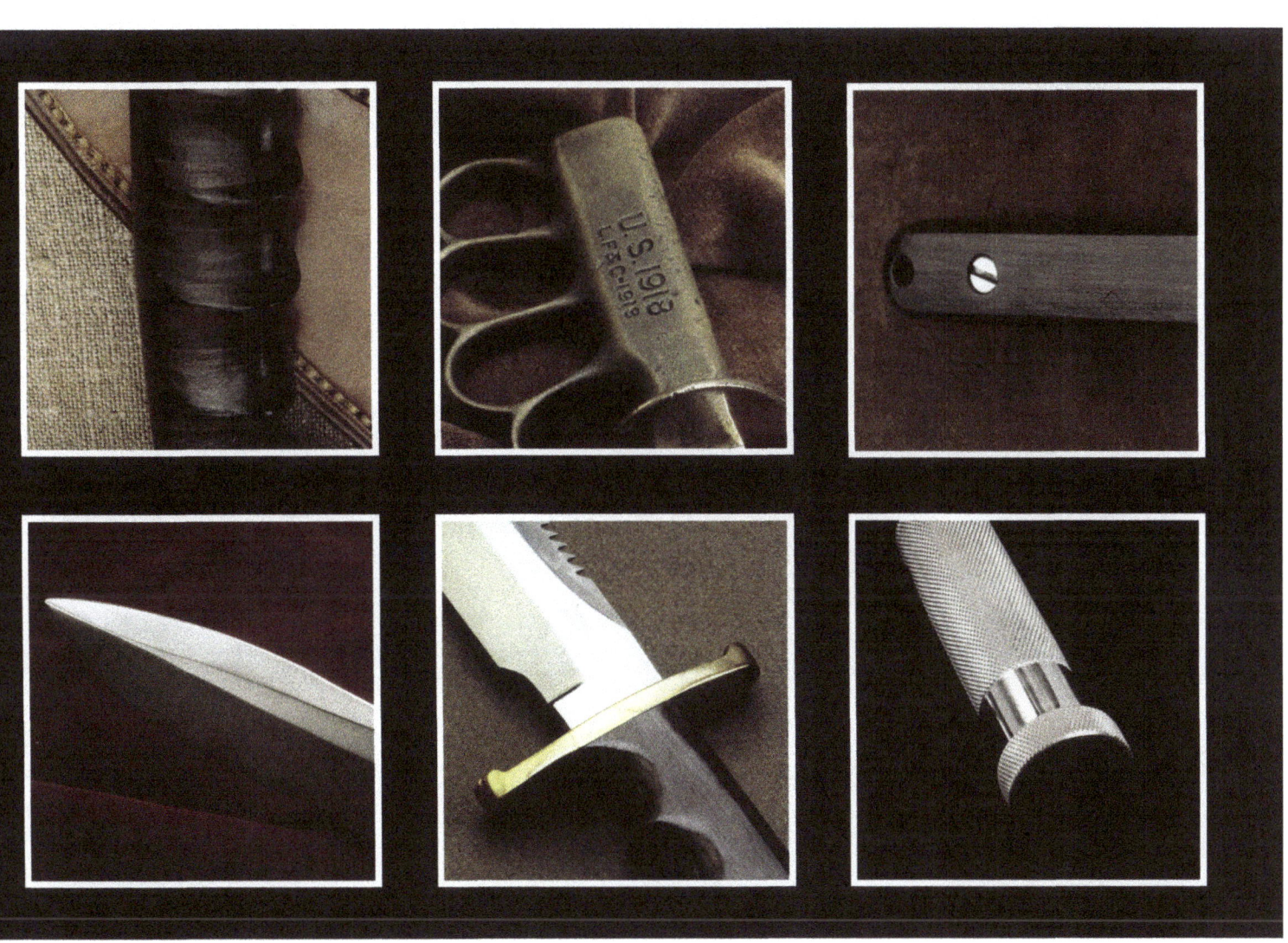

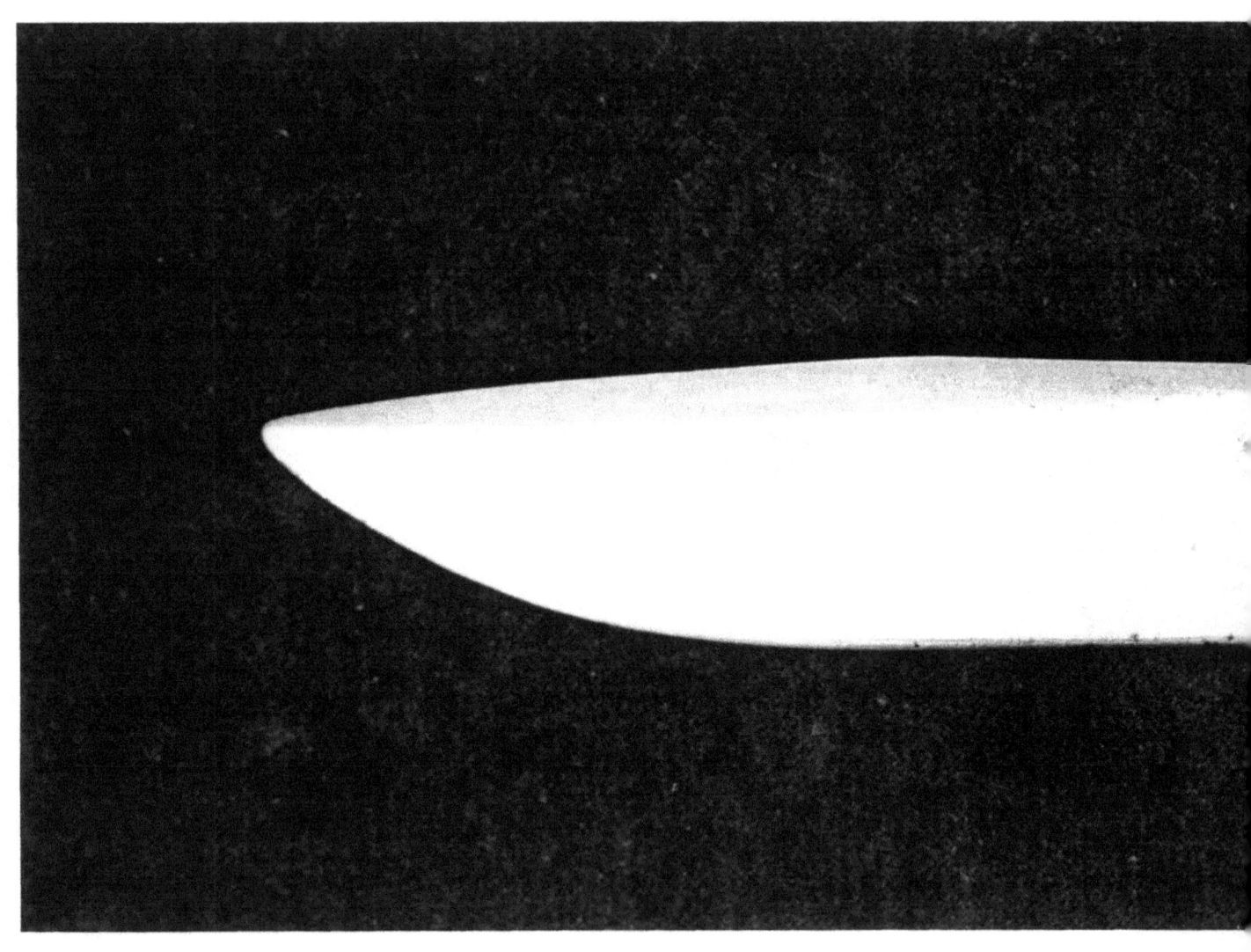

Model #1-7
Early 1940s reverse-curved upper quillon

This knife is identical to the unused fighter depicted in the previous section and from the Randall Museum, the only difference being that it reportedly accompanied a U.S. serviceman on duty in the Pacific theatre during WWII where it was exposed to field use. Opinion abounds regarding which fighter type precedes which other, but in the author's opinion, the material, spacers, guard shape and blade indicate a very early example of Bo's original fighter design. Note the thickness of the leather handle washers and the pot metal spacer at the thin butt cap. The original sheath accompanies the knife, which is a Heiser, without stamped blade or model marking on the back.

Author's collection

Model #1-7
Early 1940s
Orange/green spacer arrangement

While researching and compiling material for this volume, I formulated a long list of potential examples for inclusion. This knife continued to come to the top. It has been photographed before and made its first appearance in Randall Fighting Knives and again in a pairing in Randall Military Models. In spite of this, and because of its proto-typical characteristics, it appears again, perhaps in a more suitable setting due to its rarity. It is also a close relative to the "Benjamin" fighter with the reversed upper guard extension, whose mate resides in the Randall Museum and is depicted in the first section of this book. Although the characteristics haven't changed, perhaps the photography will provide added interest to the many collectors whose interest runs to fighters and who can relate and appreciate an early example, which was most probably "made by Bo himself."

Author's collection

Springfield Variations

The following images focus on the two types of Springfield's usually encountered, (if "types" is the appropriate term) and one other that can be classified that way but is rare, or at least not commonly seen. The author has written several articles on Springfield Fighters and has grouped the knives in roughly two categories, with the first being those partially or completely finished by Larsen himself and those fabricated by Northampton Cutlery. The distinction between the two is the quality and consistency of the finished knives, recognizable by handle and blade shape. This applies to spacer types and arrangements as well.

The Northampton example, while well used and illustrated for that reason, shows consistent finished work in the handle as well as the blade. Note both spacer stacks. What does appear to be uncharacteristic is the rearward angle of the lower quillon that is extreme for these well made pieces. For comparison, observe the following example of a mint unused Northampton Cutlery Springfield Fighter, which represents and reflects a common consistency knife to knife. Compare with the second Springfield, similarly stamped, which exhibits a shorter handle, thick spacers and a blade with a "non-conforming" grind and appears on page 118.

The "rarity" in the group is the knife with the fuller, the groove of which eliminated the original trade mark. In its place we can see a stamping at the ricasso which is shaped in the form of a dome and reads MELCHOIR over Phila. Cutlery.

Bob Gaddis (Blade Magazine, August 1997) writes, that at war's end, Melchoir Cutlery purchased surplus knives from Larsen and then altered the blades, obviously with the intention of selling them under their trademark.

There is further conjecture regarding the number of "unfinished" knives that were in Larsen's inventory, with little factual evidence available to solve the mystery. The knives reportedly "re-stamped" by Melchoir, perhaps as many as 200, are sufficient in number, however, to qualify them as a "variant" of the Springfield Fighter and so it is represented here.

Courtesy of Collector Ronnie Beckett

The final image depicted is a "like new" Springfield, which shows the knife in a state that approximates the 1943-44 Northampton type in its original condition. There is a great deal to be said about the eye appeal as well as the form of this Randall fighter facsimile, which more than satisfied the requirement to produce more fighters during a time when the demand was stronger than supply. The sheath is in similar condition, and reflects Mosser's work as a suitable sheath for such a knife.

Author's Collection

1940s Fighter & Heiser Sheath
Translucent red snaps

I like viewing this knife in the sheath, as we don't see many Heisers with "red" snaps sheathing a fighter. The translucent button was introduced during 1946, possibly as a replacement for the previously adopted "Brown button" or logo snap used on all Randall sheaths. Reorder may have resulted in the substitution of alternative snaps, which were red and the variation was incorporated.

Subsequently these buttons were used on sheaths of all models until replaced by the end of 1949*. Therefore, although not uncommon on Randall-Made field models, this was a time between WWII and the Korean War when fighting knives were not in demand, which accounts for their relative rarity on a Model #1.

The sheath has a lovely reddish-brown tone, a color that can be observed in many sheaths from this period, both hunter and fighter. Stitching is tight and there are two small rivets at the throat and a copper rivet securing the handle keeper. The stone is white. The Heiser stamp is on the rear with a "7" under the logo.

The blade on this knife measures seven inches exactly and shows excellent used condition. The stamp is full and we see the beginning of a deeper choil cut and flatter top line. The solder has been generously applied, which is typical for the period. Note the thick center spacer in the front stack, which is medium red, thin white, thick blue, thin white and medium red.

This arrangement was apparently introduced sometime during the late 1940s and was the first departure from the 5 medium-thick arrangement that we observe in mid-decade and would give way, about 1950 or so, to 3 medium-thick-2 thin. Notice, also, that the butt cap has been drilled for a thong.

Author's collection

*Note exception: Early Randall Bowie knives of circa 1953 vintage, on Moore sheaths, carry the red snaps; sometime after they had been substituted for brown buttons on all other models.

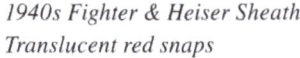

RANDALL MADE
ORLANDO, FLA.

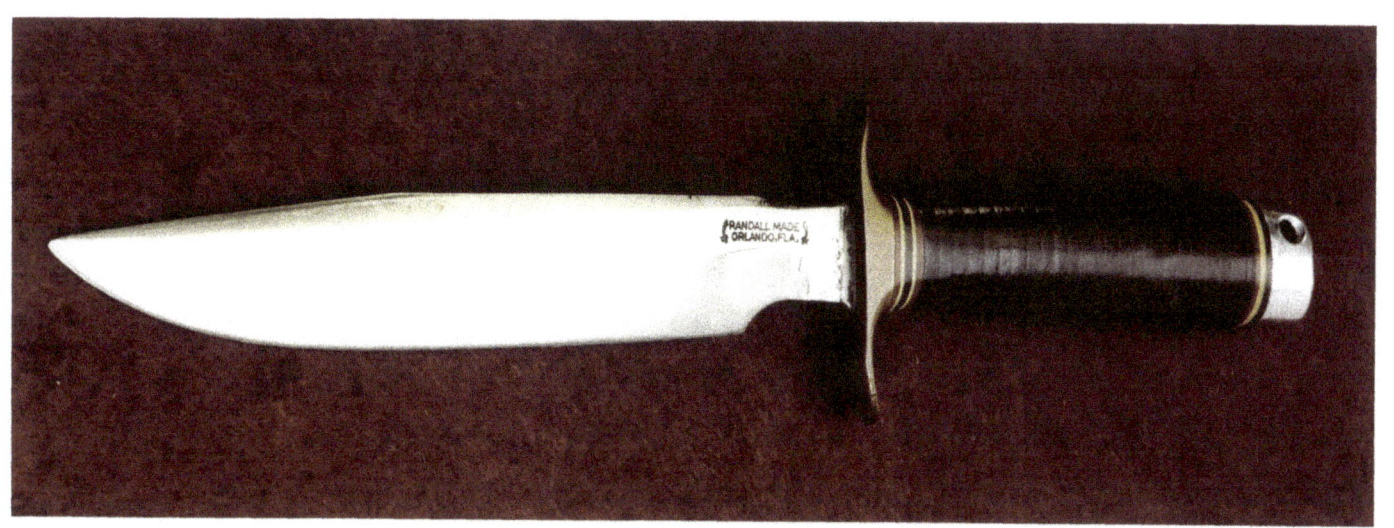

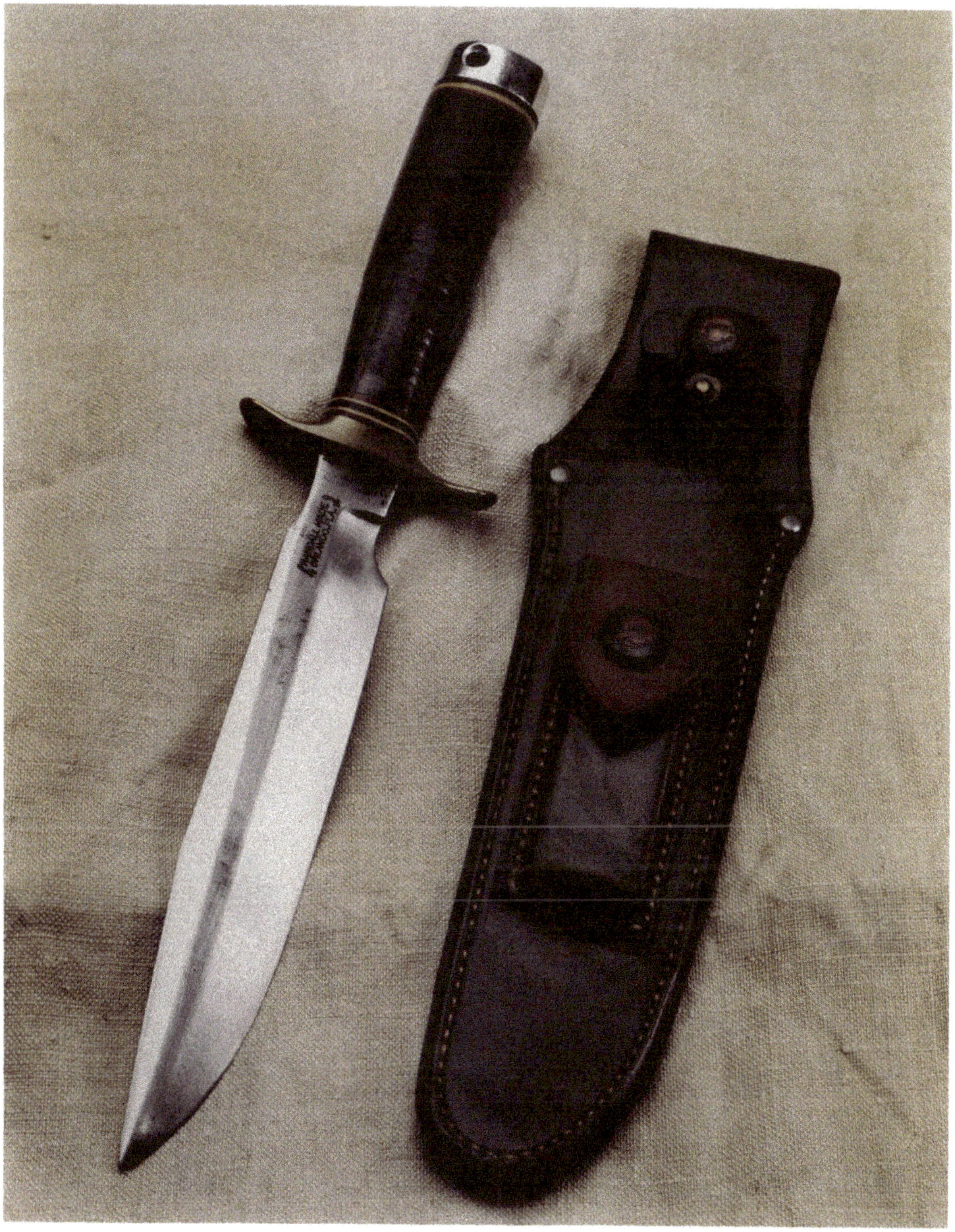

Model #1-8 1950s
Finger-grooved leather handle

It's a goal of the authors to show continuity in design evolution within specific types when there are known examples. This is one of those cases where a very early 1940s fighter, name-etched to Bo and displayed in the Randall Museum, is followed by another of the same type, illustrating the similarities and differences in the finished knife a decade later.

The former knife, depicted in Section One, may be the earliest known example with a leather finger-groove handle. The latter, also showing finger grooves in leather, is another rarity, with few examples produced during the intervening years. Bo's preferences for handle-grooves continued on through the 1950s, but are seen on stag and, to a lesser degree, in ivory. (See Randall Military Models, p. 31)

The usual comparisons can be made in blade shape (grind), but the grooved handle is quite similar. The Heiser sheath accompanying this knife is typical of early 1950s production; an excellent example, showing no signs of field use.

Author's collection

Model #1-8 Stag Fighter
Six-Spacer – mid-1950s

This is a mid-1950s example of a perfectly preserved, original condition 8-inch fighter with pinned stag handle and finger-grooves. This vintage knife has refinements not in evidence during the 1940s and yet, still reflects many functional characteristics no longer found a few years later. To many, it represents a period that produced the highest level of the maker's craft and is a very convincing, if not compelling, style of fighter.

The pinning process was still in use until the middle of the decade, but would be replaced soon after the mid-50s. The handle "drop" is a bit ahead of its time, being more universally used during the early 1960s.

The rarity of this knife is in the spacer arrangement. There are six spacers rather than the usual seven encountered on non-leather handled knives.

The sheath is "blonde" and perfect in every detail, complementing and reflecting the image of the knife.

Collection of John Cheek

Model #14-7½
Tenite Handled "Attack"

This Model #14 qualifies as "rare" due to its early production date and its present day well preserved condition. The Solingen blade with strong ricasso stamp adds to the image and the Heiser canteen snap sheath, uncommonly seen, completes the package.

When we attempt to follow the history of this model, it is easy to define the origin, but more difficult to pinpoint time of manufacture, until Johnson arrived on the scene. Early (1950s) Heiser sheathed knives and later Heiser's (1960), didn't carry dates and both knife and sheath would probably be very similar in type. This knife provides some design features that indicate 1950s, and therefore separates itself from those full-tangs produced during the early Vietnam build-up when orders finally materialized for this model. With increased production came the subtle changes in the process of its evolution, reflected in refined workmanship. There isn't much refined about this example. The tenite handle is squared-off and has a blocky appearance, the guard is fully 3½" long and the top line has a bit of a "sway-back" look to it. All in all, an example of a well preserved full-tang with many original-type design features in tact.

Author's collection

Model #14
Brown Micarta, Low "S"

The basic distinction in blade shape between the Model #18 and the #14 that preceded it, is the location of the bevel on the blade back. The crutch-tips were beveled from a point just forward of the trademark, which was an accommodation that worked for the cutting of saw teeth. Initially, "teeth" were not an option on other models. When it became available on the "Attack" models, the tip end of the blade was ground into a spear point. The knife depicted here is an early vintage brown micarta-handled #14. Observe the unique top line and the clip point tip. That's not all that is unusual about this mint example from the mid-1960s however. An "S" for stainless steel has been stamped low on the ricasso, adding to the rarity of this fine piece.

The brown micarta handle has one filled screw hole and shows the typical reddish brown wood-grain like texture of this type of material.

Courtesy of Peter Cuervo

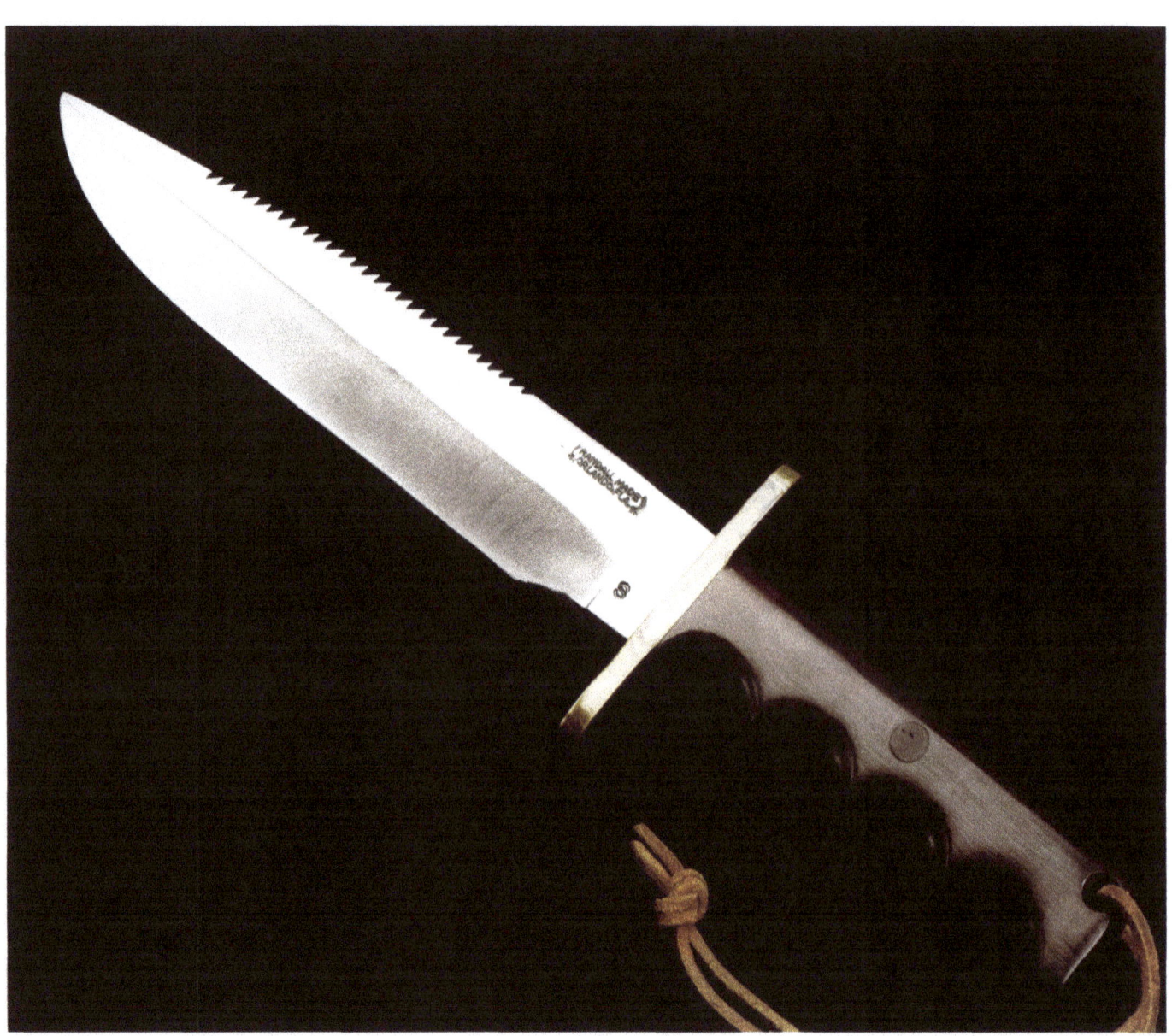

Brown Micarta Model #15
Lugged Hilt

A Model #15 with a brown micarta handle is uncommon; in stainless steel with saw teeth unusual; but with lugged hilts, rare. This knife appears in the author's first publication Randall Fighting Knives, although not to the extent that it is depicted here. Only the very earliest knives with this handle material would have a sheath with Johnson brown buttons. As is the case with many of these knives, the sheath is virtually unused and I suspect that the blade was scratched by overzealous sharpening by the owner, probably while "bonding" with the knife. Several years had passed since lugs were welded onto the brass guard, but this one still shows handwork in shaping. Their size is not extraordinary either, as the "Airman" carried a large flat guard and this fits the image. It's the blade that makes the knife in this case. This one is Orlando-made, logo-etched, also unusual and with a "separate S". Note the placement of the filled screw hole, indicating that the tang had been previously drilled in that location.

Author's collection

Model #15-5
Kit Knife

Here is an unadorned #15, with finished blade and tang, but without a guard or handle. Knives were offered for a short period of time in this condition, with the option to complete the knife by the customer who purchased it. It was an "experiment" that unfortunately led to "un shop-like" examples of catalog models circulating with inferior parts and workmanship and was ultimately discontinued. This knife, complete with drilled tang holes for handle and thong, included the bolts. Note the strong ricasso stamp.

Courtesy of Fred Stegner

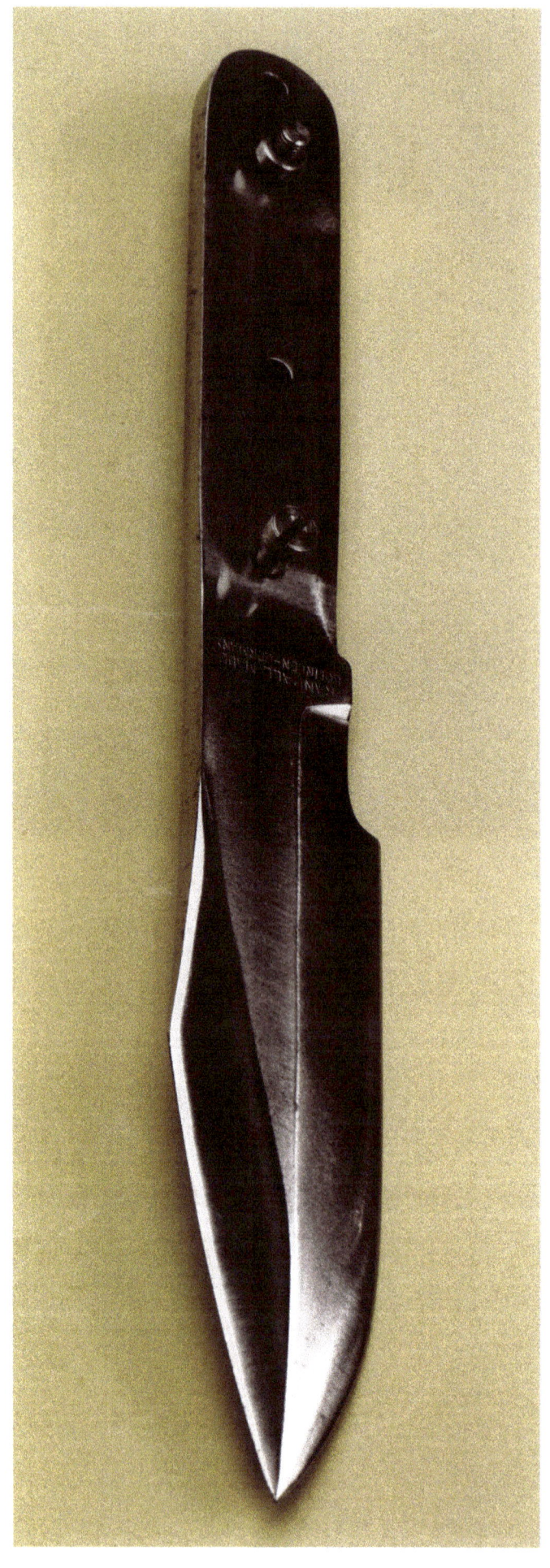

Model #16
Original type, early vintage

The Model #16 "Diver" was another example of a knife designed to meet specific customer demands. Bob Gaddis has traced the origin of this model from the Randall shop records, along with reproducing the original design sketch drawn by Bo. The first several (6-8) knives referenced in the sketch resemble the one photographed here. At least one, if not five, went to James Jones, writer of fiction and ardent diver, who made the original request. That knife has since been documented in the collection of Tom Clinton.

Full tang models, by this time frame (1958-60), included Models #14 and #15, which were first produced during 1954. Design refinements were apparent in those models by the time the #16 was introduced and it wouldn't take long to produce an enhanced version of the Diver depicted here. Note the shape of the blade on the early Diver, which measures 7¼" in length, and compare it to the aforementioned sketch. This is certainly a "heavier" type, as the original design favored. The choil cut is short and very thin. Observe the small lower extension on the guard and the angle that it presents. The upper guard extension is both short and angled forward, which accentuates the illusion of a declining angle, tip to extended tang. The shape of the tenite handle favors the "blocky" style of the earliest full-tangs.

The wax impregnated sheath accompanying the knife is the original Diver design, which was initially offered in this configuration, with ties, but without a fastener (keeper strap). The Randall trademark, model, and blade length appear between the belt loops on the front of the sheath by individual stamping(s). The author is mindful that this period was transitional with respect to sheath makers, with exact overlapping dates being inconclusive.

Author's collection

Brown Micarta Astro "1965"

The date that appears on the reverse side of this blade, 1965, was an unexplained occurrence as far as the author was concerned, until quite recently that is. With the surfacing of the Westbrook Collection, the date took on significance. Obviously this was a year of experimentation, exceeding the normal course of events that saw a more or less unbroken timeline of Randall "innovations". The knife is in the scarce category due to the handle material, brown micarta handle slabs on this model not being in abundance. Design characteristics notwithstanding, the blade shape favors the drop point that it was designed to incorporate, more so than most. The stainless guard on this knife matches perfectly the proportions of the blade and handle — slim. During this time, forging marks were not necessarily removed during grinding and polishing and they are in evidence here. Like all of the various models produced, handwork is to be seen during the early stages of production, later to give way under a more refined finishing process.

Author's collection

Ingraham-Randall Attack-Survival Knife

When George Ingraham, Captain, USA Medical Corps, sketched out a preliminary knife design for Bo Randall, he could not have known that the ultimate design would become the most popular RMK during the Vietnam era. Neither could he have fathomed the intense interest and high-end collector appeal of the surviving original.

Especially created for helicopter pilots and crew, the knife depicted here is that original Model #18, handcrafted by Gary Randall* and name-etched to the man who provided the original design features. This circumstance may be unique to this knife alone and what's more, it has survived in excellent condition, being in the possession of the original owner for many of the intervening forty years. Its place in history will be further enhanced by these photographs, as this design was to become the prototype for all of the hollow-handled survival knives that were to follow.

Interestingly enough, the genesis of this knife has been documented and published through the efforts of Bob Gaddis, including the letters written by Bo to the Captain in Vietnam. In Ingraham's response he describes the handle-wrap that was unique to this original knife and remains unaltered (accompanying documentation). Additionally, the contents in the tube appeared to have been left undisturbed and have been removed for photography.

Macro images highlight the innovative design features of this knife. The blade length is 7¼ inches, ground from Solingen steel, and the saw teeth were cut by hand, representing the first on a Randall blade. The ricasso shows a strong stamp and the reverse side of the blade is etched with the name of the owner of the first knife of its kind. Note the handle wrapping; leather and paracord are entwined, then wound and tied on the tube. The white "crutch-tip" cap is the original type and fits the handle snugly, but is easily removed. Even the sheath is personalized, as it carries the name and serial number of its owner on the back.

*Gary Randall in recent conversation with Bob Gaddis confirmed the story of his involvement in the project and reminisced about the event. At the time he was very concerned about the handle staying on, as the knife used was a full tang Model #14, and this was the first attempt at silver soldering. The full tang apparently lasted for a year or so on the Model #18, then gradually receded in the tube.

The following are excerpts from a letter written recently by George Ingraham, responding to questions about the history of this knife.

"The knife came to be designed one night when I ran across a Randall catalog one of the guys had left in the dispensary . . . and I got to sketching on an envelope. It struck me that although we had survival supplies in the helicopters, all you could really count on if you went into the trees was whatever you had tied to yourself when you got out of the bird.

See, in 1962 we weren't supposed to be combat troops; we were normally under the embassy and were supposed to be training and supporting ARVN. The 81st was designed to be attached to a large infantry unit as a support element: none of the units at Holloway were designed to be independent. For example my own outfit, the 94th Medical Detachment was not issued an individual weapon for each man.

… That meant that everybody was on his own as far as weaponry was concerned because we weren't supposed to need any.

So when I ran across this catalog I sketched up something that I thought might be useful and sent a letter to Bo Randall. He replied that it didn't seem like something he'd want to do and I figured that was that. A couple of months later a package with two knives in it showed up in the mail with a note from Randall (how I wish I had kept it!) saying that he couldn't get the design out of his head and finally made two: mine (no charge!) and one to show around and see if there was interest at (I think) the $75.00 level.

I was one of the lucky ones at Holloway: I flew a number of medical evacuation missions with that knife tied to my leg, but I never had to use it for anything. The original came home with me and I gave it to my father as a souvenir."

The credit for uncovering and bringing this rare find to the surface after so many years, goes to Doug Smith, whose recognition of its importance and persistence in acquiring it put it into the realm of the collector.

Author's collection

Model #18-7½
Full Tang

This knife features a broad, wide Orlando blade with "saw-teeth" cut and broken on the top edge in the early style, which provided a more effective cutting surface not prone to hang-up on the applied object.

Original design features are clearly recognizable on this knife, which was primarily a survival tool with multiple potential applications built into the blade, handle and guard.

The guard, of large dimensions, would permit hammering and serve to protect the hand, while the hollow handle would provide a narrow cavity for a few selected items for limited field survival use. The full tang construction, configured for strength on these early types, ran the entire length of the tube and in some instances was squared off at the end just below the cap, as in the case of this knife.

Orlando blades were sometimes found on the early examples of the "Attack-Survival" knives and represent a noticeable difference in grind from the Solingen blades when utilized on this model. Note the almost flat top line and compare with the original Ingraham knife in this section. This blade type might explain why the tang was not rounded at the end, as early "crutch-tips" were made from modified "Attack" models, where the tang was extended for a wrist thong. This example, with an Orlando blade, was obviously made with the intention of producing a Model #18 from the start.

The full-tangs underwent the usual upgrades and improvements in workmanship, which quickly resulted in the production of a more refined style. The tang was first reduced and then eliminated altogether when procedures finally permitted, allowing the entire hollow handle to be utilized for storage. The end-cap, a rubber tip manufactured for walking crutches and improvised by RMK, came in several types. This so called "crutch-tip" protected the contents of the hollow handle and lent its name to the model. It was eventually replaced by a screw cap that threaded into the tube.

This example presents all of the functionally driven features associated with the original design and is the most collectible type of this very popular Vietnam era model.

Sheaths for the Model #18s were made by Johnson, were split-back in design and used large rivets at the throat. Most have nickel-plated steel snaps on the keeper and stone pocket, with a few examples having opaque logo brown buttons. Period sharpening stones would be two-tone gray.

Author's collection

Model #18-5½ with Full Tang

The history of this knife is obscure, but the previous owner, collector John Cheek, indicated that it included Vietnam carry, although the records were lost. It is a very early example. The blade shape is distinctive and its size gives it a more "knife-like" appearance then those that were to follow by a few years. Recalling that the first hollow handled knife made for Dr. Ingraham represented the initial attempt at silver-soldering the tube to the guard and Gary Randall's first attempt at cutting saw teeth into the blade, there is visual evidence here that this knife soon followed the prototype. The reader can observe the irregular cut and "broken" teeth, but cannot readily see the solder work at the hilt. Inside the tube, which is very long at 4 5/8 inches (1/8" longer than the prototype model), we can see the rounded end of the full tang, indicating that this Soligen blade was originally intended to become a Model #15.

The sheath shows field use, but all of the buttons and rivets are intact. Brown button snaps are to be found on only the earliest examples of this model, which was introduced to the public in 1963. Like the Airman model that preceded it, the smaller size and overall dimensions made this type a very compact knife for multiple service uses and a favorite with aircrews.

Author's collection

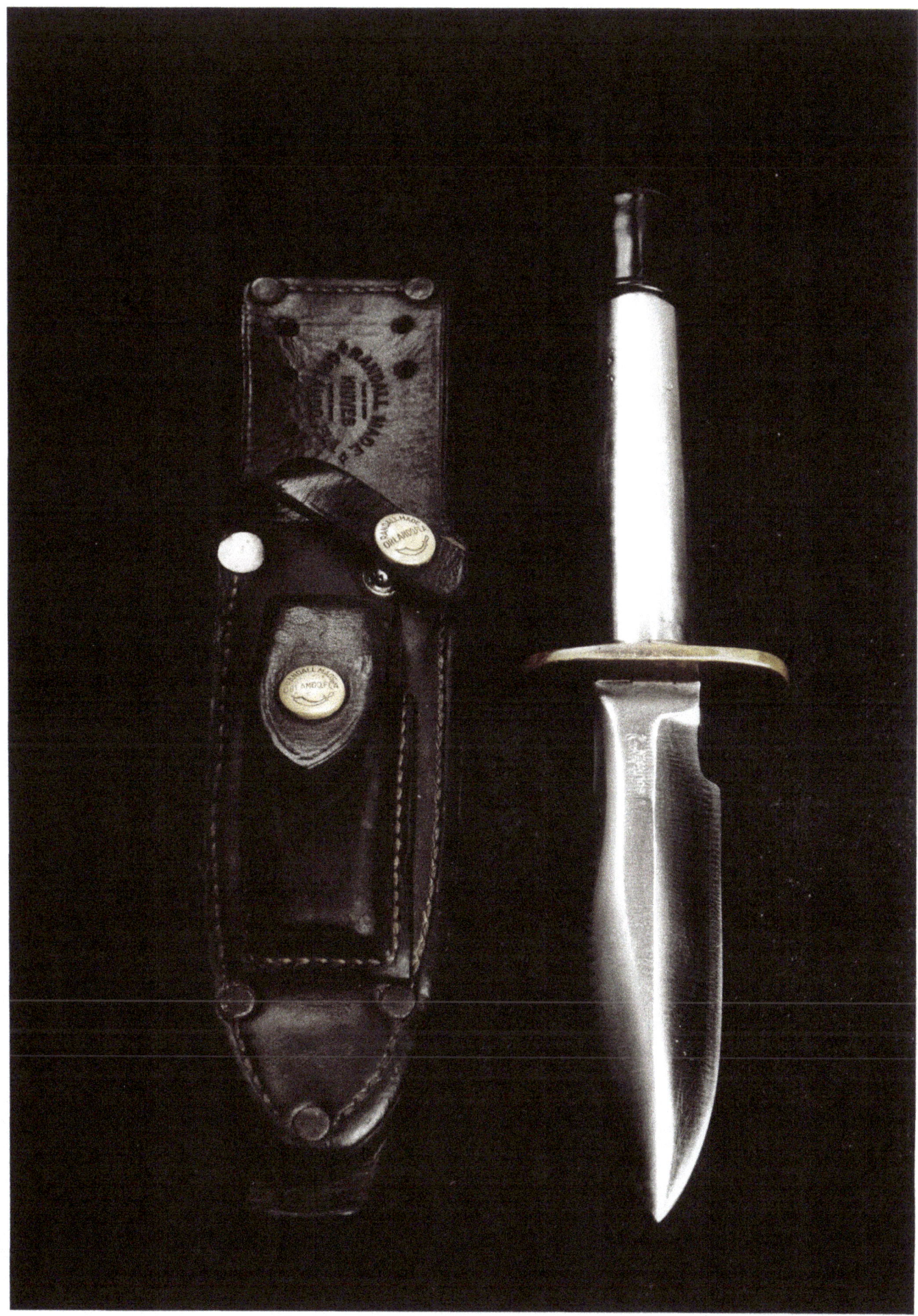

Model #18 with "Experimental tube"

This book's title reflects the content, although there are distinctions between the terms: rare, unique, and experimental. We have tried to hold the line here. This example of a late Vietnam era hollow handled survival knife falls into the third category and may also be included in the other two as well. Initial attempts at finding something like a screw cap go back to the original knife. It wasn't possible then and waiting for technology would have delayed the project for years. We don't know how many attempts were made to solve the issue of threading the narrow tube for a device to replace the crutch tip, but this example shows the completed "experiment" on at least one knife. (See Beaucant, RKS Newsletter #25).There isn't anything remarkable about the blade, but the handle is unique. Its length is 4 15/16 inches, its wall thickness a full 1/8", and it carries a tang one-third the length of the handle. The screw cap is heavy, as is the knife, which goes off my scale somewhere over twenty ounces, compared to approximately 15-16 ounces for a standard model. The cap is knurled and hand-filed, crude and uneven. It appears to be of solid brass, having a gasket to seal the tube and is adorned with an "O" ring soldered to the butt end, probably intended for a thong, making the design features of the cap quite remarkable.

Author's collection

Model #18
Leather Handle Cover

The knife is standard for its 1970s vintage, but it does have a nice option of compass in the cap and a very well constructed and stitched leather hollow handle cover to assist in gripping the otherwise smooth surface of the tube. Most probably not a shop addition, although some handle wrapping was done on early examples, it nonetheless compliments the knife and serves to exhibit an owner's ingenuity on a handle style that has given expression over the years to leather boot laces, paracord, electrician's tape and fishing line wraps, to name a few.

Courtesy of Gilbert Eckler

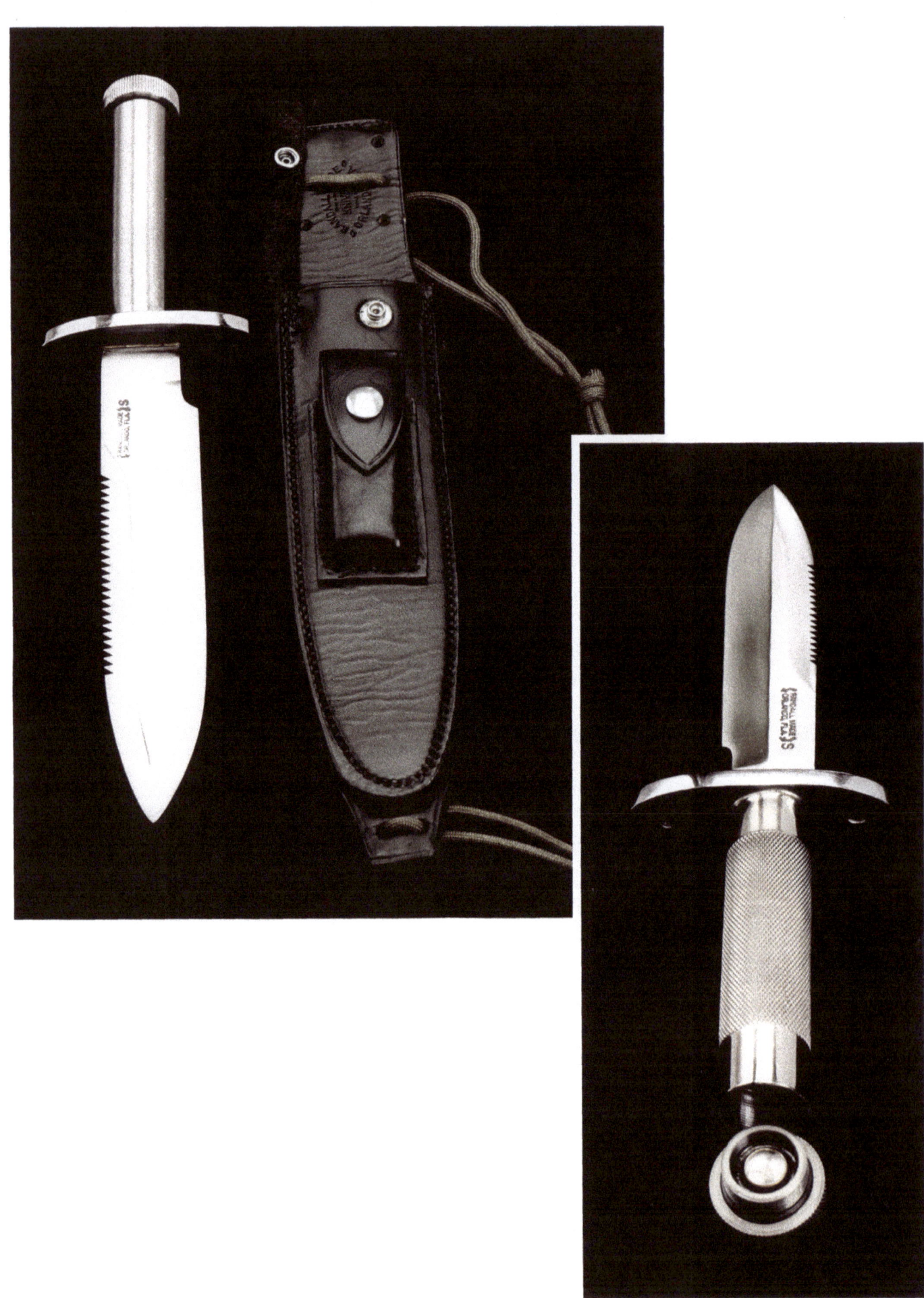

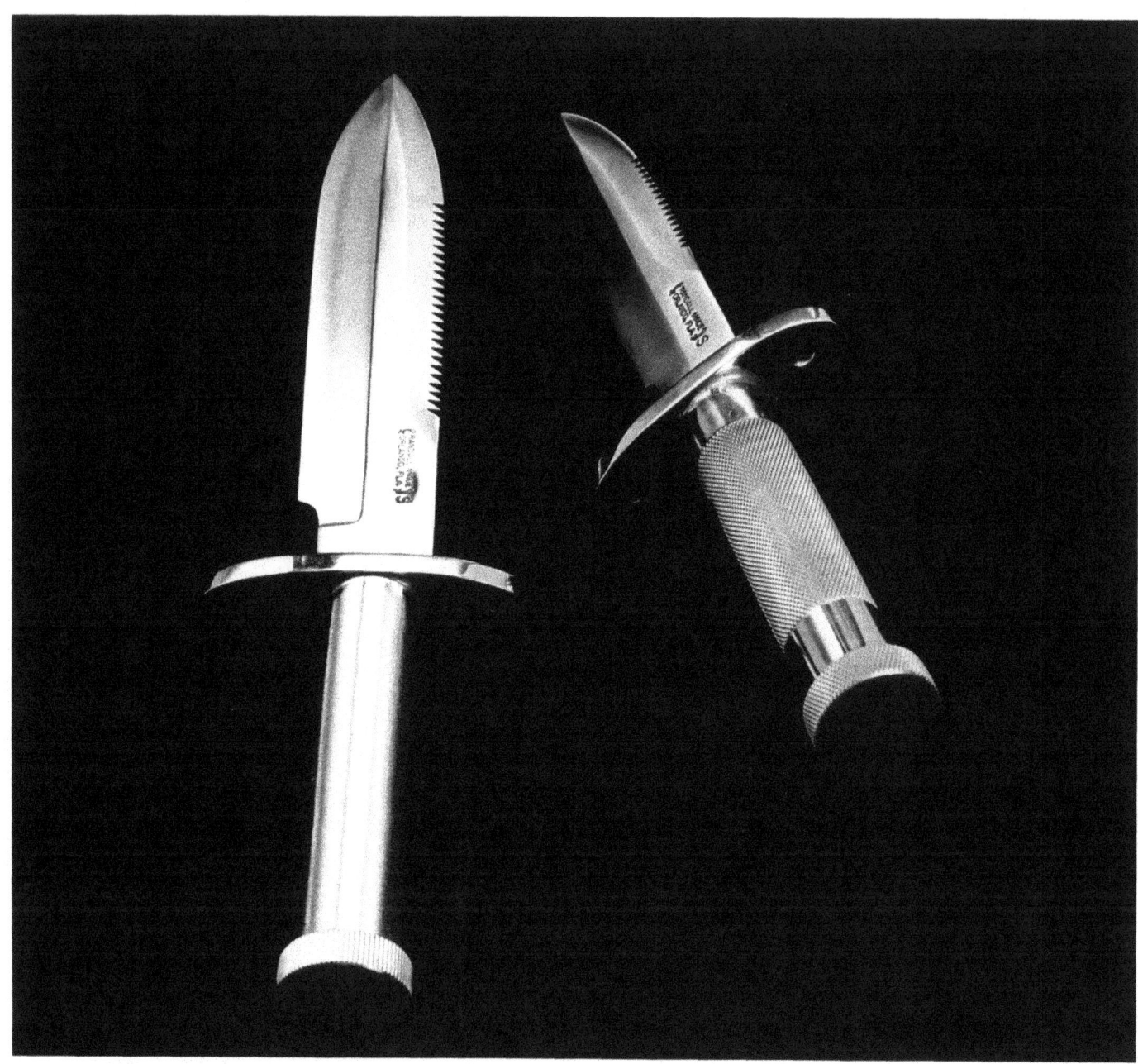

Model #18s
All stainless steel

The pair of hollow-handled knives depicted on these pages is unusually late for sought after collector's pieces. Produced during the 1970s until the late 1980s, they represent an attempt to make this "indestructible" survival knife even more suitable, if not more eye-appealing. The 7½" version has a smooth tube and a screw cap with serrations. Contrast this with the shorter knife, which has a knurled handle and handwork to match on the cap.

The first of the all stainless steel 5½" models were produced in 1976 with the same features on the other. Reportedly, the first knurling on the handles took place about 1984 and carried over to the cross cuts made on the cap as well. This example would certainly be considered scarce, as it numbered less than fifteen in total. Accompanying this is the unusual inclusion of a compass in the butt cap; another rare or perhaps unique feature of this knife.

Rarity is usually tied to scarcity and these knives are no exception. Pete Hamilton, former shop foreman, has written that less than one-hundred of the larger type exist, while perhaps fifty or less of the smaller were made. Since the manufacturing required stainless steel, it was never the intent to be a full production model, and eventually was discontinued due to problems with the butt cap locking in place. Nonetheless, they represent yet another of the many examples of Randall modifying or improvising a knife type for suitability; a practice that is identifiable throughout their impressive history.

Courtesy of Peter Cuervo

Special Stiletto
Leather Handle

This "special stiletto" with brazed brass forward curved hilt, mirrors the previously depicted images in the Westbrook Collection and those photographed at the Randall Museum. The knife blade has the same grind and stamping and appears to be made in the same thickness. The full tang handle differs in that the slabs are made from leather and are held in place with brass rivets. This would look extraordinary in a riveted sheath, but unfortunately the original did not accompany the knife where it was located, displayed on a table at a well attended gun and knife show. Leather worked as handle material for decades on fighters as well as field knives and this "experiment", although apparently not repeated, is an interesting innovation, intended to compliment the stainless steel and brass of another indestructible Randall knife.

Author's collection

Styers Fighter

Earlier, in the Randall Museum section, we depicted an image of an "original" Styers fighter of 1950s vintage. Here is a 1970s version of the same type. The blade measures 7¼" and is stainless, but without the prominent hump of the original. The grind favors the museum knife and is distinctive for that reason. Note the "S" shape of the guard with the thumb recess on the upper extension. The handle material is maroon micarta, shaped in the swelled center style with a slight drop. The Johnson sheath was obviously contoured to receive the unique hilt shape and is stamped with a 14 on the front.

Courtesy of Gilbert Eckler

WWII Fighter
(Eiler Cook, USMC)

What makes this 1945 Fighter unique is the history of the blade and the man who purchased it as a second Lieutenant during 1945. It is photographed against the book jacket, which documents its travel (and use) over the past sixty years. The accompanying letter to this author omits any reference to the professionalism and character of its original owner that I hasten to qualify as "first rate."

The knife, although carried, has been well cared for and it shows. It is nothing if it isn't typical of 1945 production. The sheath, with its original condition painted snaps, small throat rivets and "relieved" stone pocket with original stone, label and all, present the viewer with a facsimile of the knife when newly purchased. The back of the sheath is labeled with a dyno marker "USMC" and "Swede" Cook. It remains a great example of a 1940s fighter with a nice accompanying history.

Author's collection

1943 Model #1-6
"Spectre, the real reason to fear the night"

We have previously photographed two fine examples of 6-inch fighters in another publication; both with documented service connected use. As early fighters, all three differ in configuration, in spite of the similar blade lengths. The knife depicted here is a heavy looking and feeling "stubby brute" with full wide blade and a handle and guard to accommodate it. It has survived well, showing some wear and more than adequate care. The sheath is a very nice Southern Saddlery, uncommonly well made, with heavy leather, close stitching and tell-tale rivets. As is customary, it does not display a trademark. The knife is included in this book and its "uniqueness" established, through the service that it provided to an American fighting man.

The story begins, not during WWII when the knife was made, but many years later when it turned up during the Vietnam War. Bob Gorman writes the author that ". . .the knife originated around WWII with a pilot flying raids on the Formosa Islands for the Army Air Corps. He died sometime around there." The knife stayed in the Air Force and apparently "survived" Korea and then surfaced in Vietnam. Gorman relates that whoever had it, wound up flying C-130 gunships. In 1972, Captain "Ozzy" Osborn gave the knife to Bob where he states that ". . .we had several close encounters together, running covert operations in Laos and Cambodia and by now the 16th Special Operations Squadron had been established." Bob flew more than fifty missions before rotating out, but did not pass the knife down. "We didn't think the new guys had the togetherness we did."

I have included one of the "encounters" that Gorman shared with this knife, which is part of the provenance accompanying it.

"It (the knife) doesn't hold many pleasant memories for me, and stirred some old anxieties. Nothing I want to pass on to my children. It's scratched from searching for mines, opening cans, cutting wire and many other daily chores. It saved me on more than one occasion. I was in three hand to hand situations and we won. The scars on the blade (reverse side) happened on a covert operation in Laos. We were just ahead of a large group of N.V. of which we had just taken out their upper management. They were upset to say the least. Running through the jungle we found our vehicle and it wouldn't start. I popped the hood and crossed the voltage regulator, it started and we got the heck out of there. This knife served with distinction and honor, never let me down."

Bob closes by writing that "It's for sale only because lately I've been having a hard time with it all. You seemed to be worthy of owning it."

Author's collection

Model #1-8
WWII – Schafer

This is an 8-inch Fighter with a steel wrist thong link and original leather thong. The blade is slim and tapers from a slight "hump" on the spine rather than the more radical top line of earlier grinds. The stamp is full but located about one inch from the guard. Earlier production saw the logo about two inches out. This blade style becomes prominent during 1945 (see King knives, RMM). The reverse side is stamped with an inverted "3" on the ricasso, which has the appearance of having been done at the time of manufacture.

The handle shows the customary "cigar" shape, but also some taper at the guard; another indication of the transition to a more contoured configuration. The spacers are interesting as the very early thick red forward at the hilt has a thin black line in the center of the fiber; otherwise it is standard for the mid-1940s knives. The butt cap has a taper and it is secured with a steel wrist thong link that I believe to be later than the brass version used during 1943. The knife appears to have been made in late 1943. The overall condition is excellent.

The sheath is a Southern Saddlery, which can be identified by the "Mosser-like" (Springfield Fighter sheath) configuration for which it apparently served as a prototype. The stone pocket flap is contoured like a Clarence Moore sheath, but the similarity ends there. Leather on these sheaths does not measure up to the quality of Moore's product and this sheath has rivets at the throat, while Moore's do not. The condition, however, is excellent; snaps are securely fixed and stitching is strong. The stone is a Norton white that appears to be original.

The owner of this knife, Louis A. Schafer, received a commission as an Ensign in the U.S. Navy in 1942, during WWII. He then completed "Scout" and "Raider" training, as well as qualifying in Naval Combat Demolition Unit (Frogman) training at the amphibious base in Fort Pierce, Florida.

While shopping at West Palm Beach, "Bud" Schafer purchased this Randall knife for $25.00 at a local gift shop. Bud stated that the shop owner seemed to know the Randall family. He further described the knife as having a number "3" stamped on the backside of the blade, where it still can be identified to this day. His memory of the purchase included the remark that "It was a premium expense, as most quality fighting knives were priced in the $1.00 to $5.00 range."

During 1943, Bud shipped overseas with the rank of Lieutenant junior grade, and was attached to Naval Group China. While working with Chinese Special Forces, Lt. Schafer carried his Randall knife every day.

Years later, Bud's younger brother Joe enlisted during the Korean War and became an Army Medical Corpsman. Bud passed the knife to Joe and he carried the Randall throughout his tour. Eventually he was wounded in action and while being carried from the battlefield on a stretcher, he reportedly lay on top of the knife, as war trophies had a way of "disappearing." Joe was awarded the Purple Heart, returned home and returned the knife to his older brother.

Author's collection

"Galbraith Davis" WWII 8" Fighter

One thing comes to mind when I see a guard of these proportions and that is big hands! This fighter has a beautifully crafted blade of eight inches and would be a "standout" without the 4-inch guard that sets it off from the handle. Note the top grind (bevel) line that runs from the tip all the way back to the rear of the trademark. The reverse side of the blade carries the name etching as indicated above. The guard, separated from the blade by a generous amount of solder and made of steel, is thick as well as long and crafted in a similar style as the standard fighters of the period. The handle is also large, but in proportion with the hilt and measures four inches in circumference. It was helpful for me to take a step back when first viewing the knife so as to identify the dimensions in perspective. The guard alone is both longer and thicker than the full tang models that were designed a dozen years after this knife was made. In spite of these unusual dimensions, the whole knife is quite in proportion and picking it up confirms the fact. Rarity, if not uniqueness, is established by the utilization of the steel guard alone. Most probably, this abnormal configuration was generated by a customer request as indicated by the name etching on the blade.

The Southern Saddlery sheath is fully intact with a relocated handle keeper riveted in place a bit lower on the belt loop. This sheath maker never attained the exactness of detail evidenced in the Clarence Moore sheaths that served as a prototype and are recognized by their less than tight contours and loose(r) stitching, as well as the use of rivets at the throat. They were, however, a very serviceable alternative. This example shows these characteristics, but is in good carried condition with deep patina reflecting its age. The sharpening stone appears to be the original and although cracked, has been glued together and carries the Norton label. This knife/sheath combination has seen field use, but remains an excellent example of an early forties fighter in both type (exceptions noted) and state of preservation.

Author's collection

1918 Mark I Trench Knife
Randall Blade

This WWI-style Trench knife saw action in the two world wars of the twentieth century. The stiletto-type blade seems to be the one constant on this knuckle duster that was, in turn, mass-produced by many knife manufacturers and hand-crafted by custom makers. (See Knives of the U.S. Military World War II by Michael W. Silvey) The fact that they turned up again in WWII should be no surprise and it didn't stop there, as the knuckle knife regained popularity again during Vietnam. That's probably the origin of this combination which features a 7-inch Randall stiletto blade fit to an L.F&C handle. Note the narrow choil cuts on the blade.

Information regarding the quantity of this handle blade configuration is sketchy, but others are known to exist. It is, however, an "experimental" type and serves to further illustrate the continuing and diverse interest by RMK to explore every avenue of military knife design.

Courtesy of Ronnie Beckett

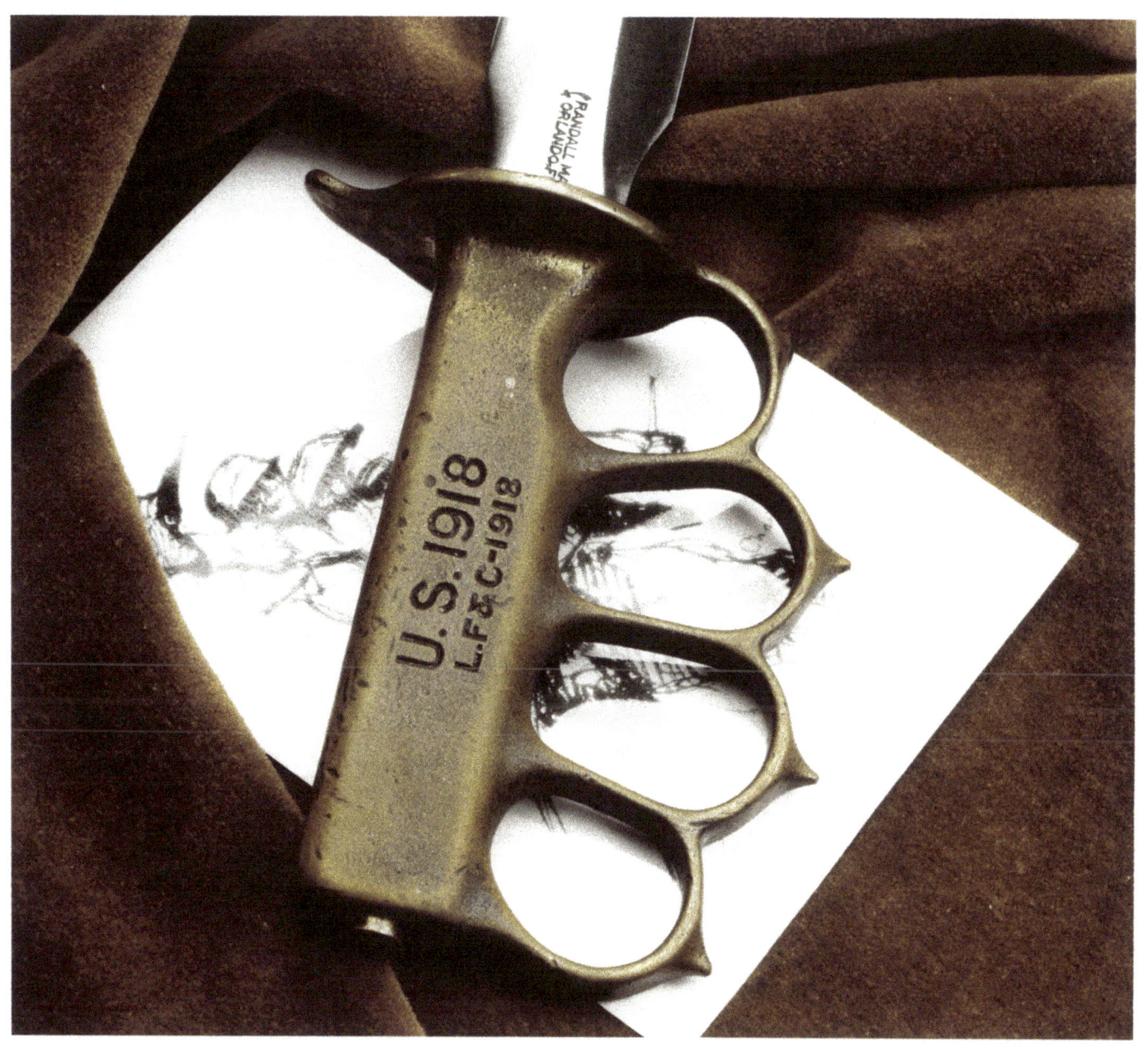

Index

Early 1940s Fighter 13

1940s Fighter; Reverse curved upper guard 14

World War II Fighter; 8" blade 17

Randall Commando 18

Styers Fighter 20

Sub-Hilt Fighter; 6" Blade 23

Special Stilettos 24

Fairbairn Ivory Stiletto 27

Full Tang Stiletto with Long Guard; 7" Blade 28

Wide Blade Stiletto; 6 1/2" Blade 31

Choiless Stiletto; 5 1/2" Blade 33

7" Carved Ivory-handled Stiletto 34

7" Malaysian Kris 37

Jade-handled Stiletto 38

Model #14 ; 7 1/2" — Prototype knife 40

Model #15; 5 1/2" — Prototype knife 41

Astro Prototype with wire clip guard 42

Astro with brass handles 43

Astro Paperweight 43

Diver with experimental handle material 45

Original Prototype for the
    Commemorative Knife 46

Randall Folders 48

Stainless Steel Fish Knives 49

Spiked Thrower 51

Engraved and Inlaid Hunter 52

Pro-Throwers 54

Early Carving Set 56

Early Stag Hunter 57

Sickle-shaped Skinner 58

Ivory Bowie set – 1950s 61

Gemini Bowie Ax 62

Full Tang 8" Bolo 65

8" Bowie, circa 1950 66

Ary Tendon Cutter 67

Kukri 69

Bear Bowie 70

Bowie knife with 8-inch blade, etched
    "ORIGINAL BOWIE KNIFE" 77

IXL Randall-Wostenholm Bowie 78

Model #12-6 Stag English Bowie 81

Model #14 with standard 7 1/2" Solingen blade 82

Model #15 with 5 3/4" Solingen blade 84

Referenced Experimental 1965 87

1-8 1/4" Fighter 88

#12-9 Sportsman's Bowie 91

#18-7 1/2" NSH – Stag handle 92

Special Stiletto 95, 96

Model 12-6 "Little Bear Type" 100

Special Stag 103

Randall Bolo 104

Hunting design 107

Model #1-7; Early 1940s reverse-curved
    upper quillon 112

Model #1-7, Early 1940s; Orange/green spacer
    arrangement 115

Springfield Variations 118

1940s Fighter & Heiser Sheath; Translucent
    red snaps 124

Model #1-8 1950s; Finger-grooved
    leather handle 127

Model #1-8 Stag Fighter; Six-Spacer –
    mid-1950s 128

Model #14-7 1/2"; Tenite Handled "Attack" 131

Model #14; Brown Micarta, Low "S" 132

Brown Micarta Model #15; Lugged Hilt 135

Model #15-5; Kit Knife..136

Model #16; Original type, early vintage 139

Brown Micarta Astro "1965" 140

Ingraham-Randall Attack-Survival Knife 143

Model #18-7 1/2"; Full Tang.................................149

Model #18-5 1/4" with Full Tang..........................150

Model #18 with "Experimental tube" 153

Model #18; Leather Handle Cover 154

Model #18s; All stainless steel............................157

Special Stiletto; Leather Handle 158

Styers Fighter 161

WWII Fighter (Eiler Cook, USMC) 162

1943 Model #1-6 165

Model #1-8; WWII – Schafer 166

"Galbraith Davis" WWII 8" Fighter 169

1918 Mark I Trench Knife; Randall Blade 173

www.ingramcontent.com/pod-product-compliance
Lightning Source LLC
Chambersburg PA
CBHW040931240426
43672CB00024B/3001